A CELEBRATION OF 100 YEARS OF SEASIDE ENTERTAINMENT

BESIDE *the* SEASIDE

A CELEBRATION OF 100 YEARS OF SEASIDE ENTERTAINMENT

BESIDE *the* SEASIDE

Bill Pertwee

COLLINS & BROWN

Acknowledgments

This book is dedicated to all those artistes who made millions of people happy in sunshine, rain and storm.

This edition first published in 1999 by Collins & Brown Limited
London House
Great Eastern Wharf
Parkgate Road
London SW11 4NQ

Produced by
PRC Publishing Ltd.
Kiln House
210 New Kings Road
London SW6 4NZ

© 1999 PRC Publishing Ltd

ISBN 1 85585 694 8

Printed and bound in China

My gratitude to those chums who responded so readily with their reminiscences and photographs: Dora Bryan, the Beverley Sisters, Max Bygraves, Jimmy Cricket and his son Dale, Pamela Cundell, Russ Conway, Bernie Clifton, Ken Dodd, Jim Davidson, Clive Dunn, Roy Hudd, Des O'Connor, Su Pollard, Tom Plummer, the Simmons Brothers, Jimmy Tarbuck and Norman Wisdom.

My special thanks to: Max Tyler (British Music Hall Soc. Historian); Terry Lomas (B.M.H.S. Group Administrator); Kenneth Shenton (Blackpool Archcvist); Brian Crompton (Leisure Parks); Peter Felgate (Eastbourne); Norman Meadow (Eastbourne); Tony Stavaker (Writer/Producer); Francis Golightly (Clacton Theatre); Norman Jacobs (Writer); David Mooney (Bridlington Historian); Michael Mills (Llandudno); Robert Holmes (Bartram Associates); Bernard Polley (Writer-Pier Theatre); Elizabeth Watson (Glasgow University Library); Dr. Sally White, Eric Joyce, Trevor Gray (Worthing); Edward Thomas (Writer Eastbourne Theatres); Peter Norris (Isle of Wight 'Footlights and Silver Screen'); Anthony Wills. Martin Easdown, Gavin Henderson (National Piers Society); Mike and Ann Paxman (Colwyn Bay Pier); Peter Elliott (Administrator 'Entertainment Artistes Benevolent Fund'); Larry Parker (Concert Artistes Association); Ken Arnott (Hunstanton); Malcolm Rowley (Somerset and West Music Hall Society); Geoff Mellor (Pom Poms and Ruffles); George Fairweather (Bournemouth); Mimi Law (Yarmouth and Boscombe); Marie Williams (Weston-Super-Mare); Ingrid Pringle (Aberdeen); Bill and Jenny Cook (Eastbourne); Billie Wiggs, Leo Bentley, Vince and Rita Starr, Barbara McAndrews, Peter Prichard Mgt (Burnett/Grainger Associates); Scott Butler (Publicity Cromer); Ivor Wynne Jones, Evan Rivers, Kathleen Cooks (Wales); Lyn Payne and Jennifer Webster, who both delivered the typing on time, every time (Horsely Secretarial Services); Dawson Strange (for photo reproduction).

My thanks also to the following tourist boards: Bournemouth, Blackpool, Llandudno, Colwyn Bay, Mablethorpe, Worthing, Tumbridge, Isle of Wight, Eastbourne, Skegness, Kings Lynn and West Norfolk, Isle of Man, Portsmouth and Southsea, Swanage and Glamorgan, and also to the Eastbourne, Bexhill, Colwyn Bay, Llandudno and Bridlington libraries, North Somerset and Bexhill Museums, and the West Pier Trust. And last but not least, my wife Marion, for her enthusiasm and help in putting the whole book together (I had to bribe her with Chinese meals). The design of the whole project is a credit to PRC Publishing (but don't tell them).

Contents

Introduction

AS AN ISLAND PEOPLE, the British have always had an affinity with the sea, but it is only in recent times in our history that the seaside has been associated with pleasure. Before that, hardy souls set forth on the briny to conquer new worlds, or to earn their living by fishing. Women would toil long hours on the foreshore gathering cockles, mussels and other delicacies to take to market or hawk the streets with the cry "cockles-alive-alive-oh'. Seaweed, rich in iodine, would be gathered by horse and cart, to fertilise the land, and when winter came the people would turn their backs on the racing tide and huddle in their little cottages, safe against the storm.

A few hardy souls had ventured, naked as the day they were born, into the sea at Scarborough early in the 18th century, but it was a Dr. Russell, seeing the potential of sea bathing for its health-giving properties, who really started the ball rolling. He claimed that bathing in the sea, and drinking the water, had medicinal benefits to cure all manner of ills and, surprisingly perhaps, it was the British monarchy that took to the idea. The aristocracy and gentry followed

This drunk was standing at the end of the pier, watching an angler trying to land a big 'un, when the angler lost his balance and fell in. 'I can't swim!' he shouted. 'I can't swim!' The drunk leaned over the edge and said, 'I can't play the piano, but I'm not shouting about it.'

in the footsteps of their royal masters — and 'the seaside' had arrived.

Resorts like Weymouth (Melcombe Regis) and Brighthelmstone (later Brighton), became fashionable because of the patronage of George III and his son the Prince Regent, later George IV. Poor mad George III was told that the climate and sea water of Weymouth would be beneficial to his health and he was persuaded to take a dip in the ocean. It was a splendid royal occasion. The naked monarch was dipped in the English Channel to the accompaniment of a band playing *God Save the King*! The local mayor was asked to show his loyalty to his sovereign,

Right: One of Catlin's early troupes at Bournemouth.

Below Right: Leslie Stacey, Easter and Vernon's 'Brighter Brighton' concert party, 1924.

Below: 'Uncle Bones' Margate Minstrels' in the 1880s.

The concert party contributed to the demise of the pierrots.

but because he had a wooden leg, he declined to go into the sea in case it rotted!

Meanwhile, 'Prinny', as the Prince Regent became known, was taking a personal interest in Brighton, building himself a magnificent pavilion in oriental style, where he entertained lavishly by night, eating and drinking to excess and repenting the next day by being dipped into the sea by the celebrated Martha Gunn, a privilege not extended to everyone. So respected was Martha as a 'dipper' that when she died she was given a magnificent funeral, and thousands lined the route. Dunking royalty had made her into a legend. Fortunately, the Royal Pavilion has been preserved and is among the many attractions that Brighton can boast of today.

Along the south coast, the small Devon town of Sidmouth had attracted another of George III's sons, the Duke of Kent. He, his wife and daughter were staying at a villa in the town when, whilst out walking on the beach in rather bad weather, he caught a chill which quickly developed into pneumonia and led to his death. The little

Alderman's minstrels played to packed houses in Eastbourne during the early 1900s.

princess, the duke's eight-month old daughter, was the future Queen Victoria. Fortunately, the villa in which they stayed is beautifully preserved, and on the sea-front is a fine hotel bearing the name of the future sovereign.

A few years later the young Princess Victoria was to visit Bognor and buy her very first pair of boots there. She bought them in a little shop very near where Butlin's is today. The shop was there until 1959, but was pulled down to make way for a roundabout! Bognor featured a great deal in the life of another king — George V. He was advised to convalesce somewhere quiet with a mild climate after a serious illness and Bognor was chosen as a most suitable place. The king recovered and the nation rejoiced. Years later, on his deathbed, he was asked if he would like to return there. In no uncertain terms he replied, 'No, bugger Bognor!' That remark cer-

tainly did not have an adverse affect on the resort, as it has retained its long popularity to this day, with its golden sands and sunshine, and it has attracted some of the best groups of entertainers at the seaside.

As the popularity of the seaside resorts grew, a demand was created for accommodation and, above all, entertainment. The crowds came and the entertainers followed. As early as 1850 there were solo performers frequenting the newly-built promenades around the coast. Musicians, acrobats, jugglers, banjoists, peanut vendors, quack doctors, bible-punchers: all tried to make a penny or two from the steadily growing numbers at the seaside. On the beach there were sand artistes, creating wonderful representations in sand of St Paul's Cathedral or Windsor Castle, ephemeral works of art that were washed away by the tide. They would be re-created the following day amid admiring glances from the children who watched with fascination the skill and patience that went into their work. (As a footnote to this, John Le Mesurier — Sgt Wilson in *Dad's Army* — portrayed a sand artist in the Tony Hancock film *The Punch and Judy Man*, filmed in Bognor.)

As the resorts grew, piers were built, first to serve the tripper alighting from the many paddle steamers plying back and forth, but later to become a promenade over the water. The element of entertainment was significant right from the start, and the promenaders were entertained by 'What the Butler Saw' slot machines and appearances by Madam Zaza, the gypsy fortune teller. Weight machines were also popular, as holidaymakers wanted to be reassured that the sea air had given them an appetite, and they had put weight on!

As the 19th century progressed however, it was the growth of the railways that gave the resorts the big boost that they needed. By the middle of the century the railways had expanded beyond recognition and vying with one another to transport the masses on holiday were many independent companies — many more than there are now in our newly priva-

A traditional concert party, whose popularity made many performers famous in their time. Arthur Askey was with 'Sunshine' for nine years.

I saw two little boys paddling in the sea this morning. One said to the other, 'Ain't you got dirty feet.' And the other one said, 'Well we never had a holiday last year.'

A typical seaside sketch

BROWN EYES

Tabs open to reveal wife and lover embracing.

WIFE: *Oh Mr Brown, it is good of you to come round to keep me company while my husband is out this evening.*

LOVER: *Darling! What time will he be home?*

WIFE: *Not until midnight; he's gone to a reunion dinner.*

BOTH: *Darling! (They embrace.)*

Tabs close
Enter husband and friend

FRIEND: *Well old boy, jolly good night wasn't it?*

HUSBAND: *Yes, great do. Pity it broke up early: still, my wife will be glad to have me home early for a change!*

FRIEND: *Charming wife you have, old boy! Such lovely brown eyes!*

HUSBAND: *Brown eyes? Are you sure? They're blue, old bean!*

FRIEND: *My dear fellow, do you mean to say say you don't know the colour of your wife's eyes? You husbands are all the same! They're brown my dear fellow!*

They exit arguing.
Tabs open on wife and lover — still at it!
Enter husband and friend talking loudly
Lover hides behind sofa.
Husband goes over to wife — looks into her eyes.

HUSBAND: My God! Brown!

LOVER: Who told you I was here?

The Pierrot troupe would set up their pitch with their backs to the sea.
A "bottler" would be sent round to collect money from the audience.

tised network. It stayed that way until 1923 when all the various companies were amalgamated into just four large ones, the London Midland and Scottish (LMS), the London and North Eastern (LNER), the Southern Railway (SR) and the GWR the Great Western, popularly known as 'God's Wonderful Railway'.

The Industrial Revolution had resulted in large concentrations of an urban workforce, who, with shorter working hours and the odd bank holiday as well, would soon be packed into special trains for excursions. The cotton spinners of Lancashire were now being transported in ever growing numbers to

Posters advertising the entertainments on offer would appear all over town.

Blackpool, Clevelys and Morecambe. Heavy industrial workers and their families from the Midlands and northeast would descend on Whitely Bay, Scarborough, Bridlington and Cleethorpes, Cromer, Great Yarmouth and Clacton. The south and southwest of England were becoming popular, too, with Londoners flocking to Southend-on-Sea, Margate and Broadstairs on the Thanet Coast and soon Bournemouth and Torquay would be within reach and increasing in popularity. The miners and the shipbuilders of the Clyde packed the trains and paddle steamers to take them to resorts 'doon the watter' such as Ayr, Largs and Rothersay. Often whole factories or yards would close for the week as it proved more economical to have the workforce on holiday all at the same time. These were known as 'Wake's Weeks', and were eagerly anticipated, as a breath of sea air in good company was more than enough pleasure for some who had never ventured further afield than the next grimy, smoky street. Blackpool not only attracted the folk from Lancashire but when the Tartan Army from Scotland arrived in town the redoubtable landladies labelled them 'Scottish weeks'. Wales was also developing rapidly, and Llandudno, Colwyn Bay, Rhyl and Aberystwyth became firm favourites with the workforce of Merseyside.

The only organised group of entertainers in the 19th century were the black-faced minstrels, complete with banjos and tambourines — such companies as 'Uncle Bones' Margate Minstrels' and Alderman's company at Eastbourne. 'Uncle Mac', who began at Herne Bay, was a much loved performer who founded 'Uncle Mac's Minstrels' in the 1890s. He took his company to Broadstairs in Kent and stayed there for 40 years. His real name was J. H. Summerson and he always worked with a black face in the style of American minstrels. So popular was he with the children of Broadstairs, that a plaque was erected in the town to honour his memory. Every afternoon at his pitch on the

Advert in *Stage* in the 1950s:
'Second comic required for Summer Concert Party, long season.
Should be able to cut sandwiches.'

Uncle Mac at Broadstairs.

sands, a children's talent contest would be held, and my wife Marion recalls entering (and winning) on several occasions, singing and dancing, with her brother John playing the piano.

Uncle Mac's troupe was the only black-faced company to survive the revolution of the pierrots led by Clifford Essex of Ireland, Adeler and Sutton from New Brighton and Will Catlin from Scarborough. Clifford Essex provided the very first pierrot company at Bray, just outside Dublin, and by 1900, Essex was operating in England. His other distinction was teaching the Prince of Wales (later Edward VII) to play the banjo! In recognition he was allowed to call his troupe the 'Royal Pierrots'.

wore their formal concert evening dress, and as they did not wish to be recognised they paraded with face masks! As they usually worked at the prestigious concert halls and smart houseboat parties on the Thames, they may have thought the seaside was a little beneath them, hence the masks, but they became very successful, and certainly enjoyed the money that they made there. However, after a few short seasons at the coasts the singers returned to more familiar ground in London.

As the 19th century drew to a close, it was quite apparent that entertainers were destined to be able to make a living at the seaside for many years to come. The beginning of the 20th century saw a more formal and organised type of entertainment and the emergence of the pierrots, descendants of the travelling players, the Comedia Dell'Arte of Italy, the story of Columbine, Harlequin and Punchinello. France transformed them into Pierrot and Pierrette and they finally ended up as part of the British seaside tradition, beloved by generations of holidaymakers.

The pierrot troupe was originally all male, composed of perhaps six or eight performers with a pianist. They would pitch their portable stage on the golden sands, well above the high tide mark, with their backs to the sea. (Forever after, a seaside venue would always be known as a 'pitch'.) One of the troupe would be given the job of going out into the audience to collect a penny or two, dropped into a

'Have you noticed how clean and spotless everything is at this resort?'
'I should say so. Even the seagulls fly upside down.'

A small group of concert singers, well-known to the Queen's Hall and Albert Hall audiences, decided to cash in on the seaside boom in the 1890s and took themselves off to the coast. They also entertained on the yachts during Cowes Week on the Isle of Wight. They had no intention of dressing up in costume, but

bottle, which would be broken after the performance and the contents shared out amongst the cast. These chaps would be called 'bottlers' and a good bottler would be literally worth his weight in gold! Incidentally if the weather was inclement they would pin up a notice: 'If wet, under the pier'.

'Wish You Were Here'

A new decade, a new monarch and new name in seaside management — the Entrepreneur

In the late 19th century a handful of performers had seen the vast opportunities open to seaside entertainment in the coastal resorts around our shores. One of them was William Braham-Fox, from Leicester, better known by his stage name — Will Catlin. He had played in a double act at William Morgan's People's Palace in Scarborough on the east coast and liked the place so much that he decided to start a Pierrot company there. This was to be the beginning of a career that was to last 60 years in many forms and in many resorts around the country.

The growth of seaside entertainers in the early years of the new century reflected something of a social change in Britain. Encouraged by the lifestyle of the new monarch, Edward VII, Britons were throwing off the shackles of Victorian dourness and beginning to enjoy the fruits of Victorian prosperity. The new king's visits to the theatre, to Cowes week in the Isle of Wight, and his invitations to entertainers to join him at his royal residences, all made for a more relaxed way of life — mainly for the upper-

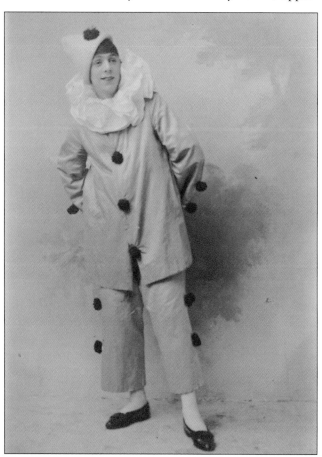

George Royle's 'Will-o'-the-wisps'.

Far Left: An early pierrot — Harry Mitchell Craig.

Left: Catlin's 'Royal Pierrots' drew big crowds wherever they played.

Below Left: Poster for the Grand Pier Pavilion, Weston-super-Mare, 1906.

Right: George Royle's 'Imps' from which the 'Fol-de-Rols' were formed.

middle classes with enough money to enjoy it to the full, but this would percolate through to all walks of life.

Scarborough, where Will Catlin would start his career, was one of the first spa resorts. The local spring waters were claimed to have healing properties and the result of this publicity added to the resort's popularity. Catlin could see that the large workforce employed in the Yorkshire mills and in the heavy industries of the north-east was now taking advantage of the easy access to the seaside provided by regular rail excursions in the summer months. All levels of society were now able to experience the happy-go-lucky seaside atmosphere that up to the turn of the century had mainly been enjoyed by the wealthy.

Catlin organised troupes of pierrots — each usually of six to eight performers — to play on the beach at Scarborough three or four times a day. He was also one of the first performer/managers to engage in public relations and advertising. On saturdays — the change-over day for holiday-makers — Catlin and his troupe, in full costume, would drive round Scarborough in wagonettes making sure newcomers were aware of the entertainment they could enjoy 'beside the seaside'.

This cavalcade would pay several visits to Scarborough station on its way round the town and Catlin would talk

to the folk who had just got off the trains for the start of their holiday. He always insisted on his troupes dressing and making up in their lodgings before each performance, so that when they walked through the town to the pitch on the sands, this would also bring them to the attention of the public. He was one of the very first to have post-cards printed with a picture of the troupe; these were sold before and after a performance.

Holiday-makers sent these postcards back to their families and friends telling them they had arrived safely and were having a good time — 'The lodgings are com-fortable, wish you were here' — and at the same time publicised the troupe.

Catlin's first pitch was on the sands under the spa wall and he didn't have things all his own way. There was con-siderable competition for the best beach pitches, mainly from Tom Carrick and his pierrot company, who had arrived in Scarborough just before Catlin. Other competi-tors included Sidney James's 'Strolling Players'. However, it was Catlin's pierrots who drew the biggest crowds. The local council, aware of this, put the rent up whenever he reapplied for a pitch.

By 1906 Catlin decided the rent was just too high and so he bought some land near the seashore and put up a stage with a canvas top. He called it 'Catlin's Arcadia',

Catlin's original pierrots on the sands of South Bay, Scarborough.

and it was to prove the beginning of a move into in a much bigger level of business. By now Catlin had become a commercial entrepreneur with business activities all round the coasts of Britain. He had arranged for troupes to play at Great Yarmouth managed by and including his brother Tom Catlin. He also had troupes at Whitley Bay, Bridlington, Colwyn Bay and Llandudno in north Wales, and had moved south to Bournemouth, too.

Others were entering this marketplace in the prewar years: a new name to arrive in Scarborough during the period was George Royle and the 'Troubadours'. When he arrived in Scarborough from Blackpool, he changed the name of his troupe to the 'Imps' or 'Will-o'-the-wisps'.

Royle was a very successful beach entertainer and when Scarborough council decided to build Floral Hall, which opened in 1911, it was Royle who was invited to provide the entertainment. Royle decided that the venue deserved a bigger and better production than his 'Imps' could offer, and so formed the 'Fol-de-Rols', taking the

Left and Below: A typical programme of songs by the 'Lancashire Lasses'.

PROGRAMME

ARTISTES:

MADAME PARSONS and her Seven Daughters,

THE

LANCASHIRE LASSES

The only Seven Real Sisters on the Stage.

SUPPORTED BY

GEORGE PARSONS & JOHN DIXON
(The Bone, Bass)

HORACE V. NEWTON   CHAS. W. PARSONS
The Clever Pianist.   Boy Vocalist.

HARRY TAYLOR, Speciality Dancer.

AND

PA PA PARSONS

MAGGIE

Corner.	6. Kingdom within your Eyes
	7. Anytime You Want Me
	8. For One Sweet Day
Violets	9. That Wonderful Mother of Mine
he Rose	10. Old fashioned Sweetheart
	11. Extra

DOLLY

1. I wonder what it feels like to be poor	7. Impressions
2. I'm getting my own back now	8. Roses and Radishes
3. Pet of the Pier	9. My Beastly Eye-glass
4. Priceless Percy	10. She Shops
5. My Word	11. When I get my Bolshevik Blood up
6. Peacetime Percy's back in Piccadilly	12. Sammy, the dashing Dragoon

EVA

1. Mammy o' Mine	15. Every day you're away means a tear-drop
2. Sorry I made you cry	16. Bye-lo
3. You can't buy a Thousand Rays of Sunshine	17. The Rose of Alabam
4. There's a Rose in Repose	18. Can't you hear me calling, Caroline
5. You can come back to me	19. I left my Heart in Maryland
6. That Soothing Serenade	20. Come down to Bungalow Town
7. Kentucky H me of Mine	21. There are Smiles behind the Tears
8. Bless my Swanee River Home	22. Lu, La' Lu
9. I'll sing you a Song about Dixie	23. You'll never miss that old Home Town of Yours
10. My Hawaiian Maid	24. I want to see my Country Home again
11. I'd no idea I'd care for you	25. Your Voice
12. They'll never know me in Old Dahomey	26. Extra
13. All that worries me	
14. You made me happy for a while	

Violin Solos.

1. Phantom Melody	6. Where my Caravan has rested
2. Intermezzo from Cavalleria Rusticana	7. Your Voice.
3. Simple Aven	8. Just a little Love
4. Il Trovatore	9. Salut de Amour
5. Until	10. Absent
	11. Extra

LOUIE

1. Dance along with a Song	12. When Night Shadows are Falling
2. Dreams of Long Ago	13. In a Red Rose Garden
3. The Garden of my Heart	14. Old Fashioned Mother of Mine
4. Sing me a Song of the Morning	15. When you look in the Heart of a Rose
5. Somewhere, Someone is Calling	16. How can my Heart forget
6. The Flower of Love	17. The Waltz is a Dance of Love
7. Love in Lilac-time	18. The Song of my heart
8. Land of Beginning Again	19. Give me the Open Road
9. Someday when the Sun is Shining	20. Your Wonderful Eyes
10. Wedding in Fairyland	21. Extra
11. Little White Hill of Dreams	

ALICE

1. I've got my Captain Working for Me now	8. She must be a Wonderful Girl
2. Wherever the Girls are	9. Where's the Girl you had Last Year
3. The Women are Wiser than Me	10. Keep 'em Guessing
4. You'd be surprised	11. If you want to keep the Boys at Home
5. Where did you find the Lady	12. Everything is Bonnie up in Scotland
6. Take your Girlie to the Movies	13. Oh! La-la, "Oui Oui"
7. When the last Colonial Soldier goes away	14. Extra

MONA

1. Father got the Wind up	10. Rachel my Girl
2. I'm a Good Girl now	11. Nobody Taught Me to Love
3. I hope it keeps fine for Mother	12. Everytime he Kissed her
4. Baby Brother	13. Stop it John
5. Oh! Billy	14. Abe, my boy
6. Any Girl from Anywhere	15. You would, you know you would
7. I'm for ever blowing bubbles	16. If you'll love me, as I love you
8. It must be You	17. Extra
9. N'everything	

Monologues.

1. Spotty	4. Only a Blinded Soldier
2. Green Eye of the Little Yellow God	5. Proposals
3. Drama of the Sea	6. Extra

HORACE V. NEWTON, S.M., L.C.M.

SOLO PIANIST AND ACCOMPANIST.

GEORGE

1. I must be Married by 12 o'clock to-night	4. Like no other Girl
2. I'm Bashful when Bathing in the Briny	5. If you want to make a hit with the Ladies
3. Everybody wants the Key to my Cellar	6. You can't fool around with the Women

The 'Waterloo Pierrots' at Bridlington in 1912.

title from 'Fol-de-rol Laddie', an old English folk song.

Royle dressed the 'Fol-de-Rols' in Victorian style costumes in light-brown basic colours. The shows were an immediate success, but only for a short time: the declaration of war in August 1914 put an end to entertainment at Scarborough, as it did to all the resort, for four and a half grim years.

Bridlington, on the north-east Yorkshire coast some 18 miles south of Scarborough. It had grown up from the small fishing village of Burlington Quay and boasted a Theatre Royal as long ago as 1800. In the 20th century, the lovely Victorian Spa Theatre played host in 1911 to

Below: Herr Julian Kandt's Band at Bridlington in 1910. Second from the right, seated, is Henry Wallace Hartley who left Kandt to take over the orchestra of the *Mauretania*. In 1912 he would become orchestra leader of the *Titanic*. On that fateful night in April, on its first voyage, he and his players showed great courage, playing as the ship slipped beneath the waves.

Catlin's 'Royal Pierrots' and other troupes such as the 'Waterloo Pierrots', who not only played on the sands but, when the tide came in, played in front of boarding houses, bottling (passing round the bottle for payment) the customers who frequented them.

Many concert parties were booked at Bridlington's new Grand Pavilion and the Spa Royal Hall before World War I, and since then practically every top-line British entertainer of this century has, at one time or another, contributed to Bridlington's seaside entertainment. In 1931, it must have been a great coup for the town when Paul Robeson, the famous American singer, performed there. Robeson's extensive repertoire concluded with his singing of 'Old Man River' from *Show Boat*, the song for which he will always be remembered.

Across the Pennines on the west coast of England, **Blackpool** and its surrounding areas of Cleveleys and Lytham St Anne's has offered visitors a wider range of entertainment and theatrical talent than any other resort in the country for over a hundred years.

Two of George Royle's 'Troubadours'.

Above: Blackpool's South Pier began life as the Victoria Pier in 1893 with a blaze of glory, bands playing, choirs singing, and in May of that year there opened the Grand Pavilion and some 36 shops. Also included was a 40-piece orchestra.

Right: George Royle's 'Troubadours' at Blackpool in the early 1900s.

Sea-end of Bognor Pier in the early 1900s.

'Uncle Tom's Cabin' on the north shore was the late 19th century forerunner of Blackpool's immense entertainment industry. Many a minstrel troupe entertained there and it benefited from a liquor licence: dancing was very popular and the odd glass or two encouraged the dancers 'to get a little closer to one another' as one observer put it.

Unfortunately, coastal erosion caused 'Uncle Tom's Cabin' to fall into the sea at the turn of the century — and by then there were many entertainment centres in Blackpool ready to take over. One of them — the Raikes Hall Park Gardens and Aquarium, which had started in 1871 and later become the Royal Palace Gardens — was probably the first theme park in the country.

The number of theatres in the resort throughout the century is truly amazing. The first proper theatre in Blackpool was the Theatre Royal — now Yates's Wine Lodge and Tivoli Cinema — which opened in 1862, presenting Victorian melodramas.

The Borough Theatre opened its doors first in 1877, becoming later the Borough Bazaar, and then Bannister's Bazaar. It would reopen much later still as a music shop run by the song-writer and publisher Bert Feldman. Feldman's became famous as a home of popular music, with a pianist sitting in the open shop window plugging the hit of the day. When Feldman finally moved his very successful business to London's 'Tin-Pan Alley', he sold out to Jimmy Brennan, a northern entrepreneur, who renamed it the Queen's Theatre. Brennan brought all the top acts to the theatre during his occupancy but it is no longer open today, the site now lying under a department store.

The Alhambra Theatre — built in 1899 on the site of the Prince of Wales — suffered a similar fate. Redesigned and reopened as the Palace in 1904, it was demolished in 1961, and its location is now the site of John Lewis's Blackpool store. Another venue that went through a variety of names and mixed fortunes was the Prince's Theatre. It became the Empire, then the King's, next the Hippodrome and, finally, the A.B.C.

The Winter Gardens (built in 1878) added the Pavilion Theatre in 1882, and in 1889 a new opera house was added to the complex, designed by the prolific Frank Matcham: many of his theatres can still be seen all over Britain — including Blackpool's Grand Theatre, which opened in 1894. The old Winter Gardens Pavilion was transformed into the Tower Ballroom, where 'Mr Blackpool' himself, the organist Reginald Dixon, was resident for years.

The pier theatres are perhaps the best-remembered of all Blackpool's theatrical venues. The Central and South from the start featured pierrot troupes and concert parties such as Bobby Allandale's 'Premier Pierrots', Fred Walmsley's 'Tonics' and the 'White Coons'. Sam Hague's Minstrels were also popular in the area, as were Adeler and Sutton's companies who played for several seasons. George Royle's 'Troubadours' played the piers, too, before he moved on to Scarborough. The owners of the North Pier always tried to provide a slightly better class of entertainment, with orchestral concerts and solo artistes from inland city halls. They invited 'Society Concert Party Entertainers' to perform in 'the new and unusual Indian Pavilion' on the pier at that time.

Blackpool's famous tower was completed in 1894 and built after the style of the Eiffel Tower in Paris. The original company could find little support for the shares they had on offer, as few thought there would be anything but a meagre return on their investment. However, one man saw a bright future. He was Alderman Sir John Bickerstaffe and he bought up all the available shares in 1894. The tower eventually cost £300,000 to build — an immense amount of money at that time — but in 1896 the company made a net profit of £30,000 for the year: not bad for starters! As well as the actual tower structure, with its wonderful hydraulic lift, within the entertainment complex was a circus, an aquarium, a menagerie, a ballroom with sprung floor and catering facilities, all in the most luxurious surroundings.

The success of the tower made the other venues aware of the need to improve facilities for the ever greater number of visitors. The influx to Blackpool had started in the middle of the 19th century with the coming of the railways. Although a line from Preston to Fleetwood had opened as early as 1840, Blackpool had to wait until 1846 when the first train puffed into Talbot Road Station and the masses began to arrive.

All this was only the beginning: as Al Jolson, the great American entertainer, once said, 'You ain't seen nothin' yet!' Blackpool's full story will be examined in the next chapter.

Morecambe has sometimes suffered from its proximity to Blackpool, but was never the poor relation, and has a long history of seaside entertainment. Morecambe played host to many pierrot companies — outdoors and

Mrs. Parsons and the youngest of the 'Lancashire Lasses' — Mona.

indoors — and before the turn of the century there was a real Negro troupe who performed on the sands. Morecambe's Central Pier was the venue for pierrots, the West End Pier preferring concert parties.

The Central Pier theatre was built as a replica of the Indian Taj Mahal and was for several years — until it burned down in 1933 — the home of Ernest Binns' summer shows. Binns was originally a light comedian with the Wavelets Company, as well as being in management. He and his entertainers stayed in Morecambe at the wooden Arcadia building after the pier fire.

The West End Pier Pavilion lasted an even shorter time: it was destroyed by fire in 1915.

One of the well-known troupes to appear at Morecambe at that time was Charlie Parsons' 'Little Lancashire Lasses' — all seven of them were his daughters, managed by his wife. She started just before World War I, continuing with the troupe when Charlie was away in the army After war, in 1919, Parsons couldn't continue with the 'Lancashire Lasses' — his daughters by then had grown up and got married. So, he formed another troupe that continued the family theme: the 'Smilers' included his two sons and one of his daughters-in-law, Beattie Pollard. They appeared on the sands near the old jetty for several seasons and ensured that no visitor to Morecambe in those days would forget the Parsons family.

Another famous name in the northern resorts had its origins in a small group of pierrots, who tried their luck entertaining the public on the promenade at Weymouth in Dorset just before the turn of the century. The troupe was led by Edwin Adeler and included a piano on a trolley allowing their pianist to accompany them in their comic songs. They did not have much suc-

Above and Right: Charlie Parsons (inset) All-Ladies Concert Party. The idea worked well until the war, after which the 'Lasses' had grown up, got married and moved away.

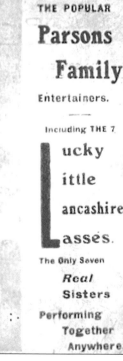

THE POPULAR

Parsons

Family

Entertainers.

Including THE 7

Lucky

Little

Lancashire

Lasses.

The Only Seven

Real

Sisters

Performing

Together

Anywhere

A very young Jack Hylton.

cess at Weymouth and they moved on to **Southport**, in Lancashire, where they trundled up and down the promenade and were joined by Bill Sutton — the beginning of a very successful partnership between Adeler and Sutton.

The troupe started to gain a following and moved from the promenade to the large garden of an empty house on the front. They only did one season there as the new house owner didn't fancy having three daily performances on her front lawn — understandable, I think!

The now firm partnership of Adeler and Sutton's Pierrots moved to Harrogate in Yorkshire for a short time before moving back to the west coast, to New Brighton in Cheshire where the 1900 season ran from early summer until Christmas — a quite phenomenal run at that time or at any time for a pierrot show. The New Brighton Pier Pavilion was taken over by Adeler and Sutton in a syndicate with Paul Wills and Wallis Arthur. They regularly invited guest artistes to perform in their shows; many of these artists would become prominent in seaside entertainment in the future.

Adeler and Sutton's fame spread quickly, and soon they had pierrot companies in many towns — Blackpool, St Anne's, Southport, Rhyl, Llandudno and their base in New Brighton. The firm of A&S used many innovations during this time, including engaging a female performer; up until then Pierrots were all men.

Their success continued until they left New Brighton and went to the Isle of Man. While initially successful on the island with a mixture of well-known names from the music halls and straight theatre performing alongside them, after disputes with the proprietors of their venue they moved to the Palace Gardens at Douglas. Here their show faltered in the face of competition from a well established entertainment at the Villa Marina.

In 1909, as the Adeler and Sutton empire appeared to have had its heyday, Edwin Adeler decided to change course once more and moved on to new horizons — South Africa to try pioneering concert parties on the African continent. Their partnership had been very successful and Edwin Adeler had been a great influence in the summer entertainment business. Amongst his achievements, he was the first proprietor to pay a guest artiste £100 a week — a considerable wage for 1908. Before he left Britain Adeler gave most of his business interests to his friend and fellow performer Bobby Alandale. Bobby was then

Below: Pierrots at Southport, 1904.

'Look out! The tide's coming in.'

married to Billy Burke, a wonderful musical comedy star here and in America who would later marry American impresario Florenz Ziegfeld.

Scarborough, so important in the early years of this century to seaside entertainment, was in a way responsible for another story that began further down the east coast in **Skegness**, Lincolnshire. The Clements family — father and two sons, Fred and Bob — worked for the Great Northern Railway at King's Cross in London. Fred and Bob started amateur concerts for their working colleagues at railway social clubs, wearing pierrot costumes they'd made themselves.

One weekend in 1901 Fred took a day excursion to Scarborough where he saw a pierrot show on the sands. Fred came back to London and having decided his future was not on the railway and that he wanted to take a chance as a professional show proprietor. He had noticed that holiday-makers from the midland towns of Nottingham, Leicester and Derby were going to Skegness for their summer holidays in ever-increasing numbers on the growing railway daily excursions. In 1902 Fred applied to the local council for a pitch and was granted one on the foreshore. He got a local builder to build a wooden stage (with a dressing room), formed a small com-

pany — a pianist, comic singer, lady soprano and Fred himself — and at Whitsun began his career in seaside entertainment.

The troupe was a flop. The crowds ignored Fred in favour of the already established entertainments — the so-called 'Nigger Minstrel' shows and pierrot companies. Fred didn't even take enough money during the first week to pay the pitch's small rental fee. Undaunted, Fred resolved to continue. He was lucky to meet an experienced professional comedian who gave him some good advice. His small group of middle-aged performers, as professional as they were, just didn't have the appeal to attract the younger audiences; what Fred needed was a larger group of good-looking young men who would attract, for instance, the girls from the Nottingham lace factories.

Clements set to work, auditioned several artistes and was all set to go again but he couldn't get a pitch from the council. He went to the Earl of Scarborough's agent, who managed some land for the earl in Skegness, and was able to negotiate a site by the pier — perfectly placed to afford those sitting on the pier a good view of the show. He acquired some long bamboo poles with nets on the end and made collections that way.

Right and Above Right: Fred Clements' middle-aged performers just did not attract the the younger audiences at Skegness in 1902. He would eventually buy a piece of land in nearby Mablethorpe and build the Victoria Pavilion.

Left: The Earl of Scarborough owned land in Skegness and was responsible for opening up the resort to the railways. He formed a company to build a pier, and this was opened in 1881. It had a fairly large concert hall, and refreshment rooms were added just before the turn of the century.

CLEMENTS CONCERT SKEGNESS

Pierrots, Mablethorpe

CLEMENTS

The pier, Clacton-on-sea, 1909.

Things started to gather momentum, but the weather did pose a few problems, though only the odd show or two was cancelled. However, he realised that there was scope for evening performances so asked one of the hotels, the Bass Breweries Hildreds, if he could pitch his troupe on their lawns at night. They agreed to this, enabling him to provide alfresco style morning and afternoon shows and nightly ones as well. After having to move his pitch a few times during those early years, he decided to branch out to nearby Mablethorpe where he bought a piece of land and eventually built a fairly permanent building, the Victoria Pavilion. Fred ran shows there for several years at the same time keeping his connection going with Skegness.

In 1911, in co-operation with Bass Breweries, a cinema was built on the lawns of the hotel. Silent films were beginning to attract audiences, and Fred was asked to run the new cinema, giving him a new outlet for his energies, particularly as he'd lost his evening venue on the lawns. He then bought another piece of land and had built the Arcadia Theatre which opened in 1912 Fred Clements now had his own theatre and evening performances were back on the menu. He also built his own cinema, the Tower picture house, after Bass Breweries decided to part company with him.

By this time Clements was also producing pantomime companies for various towns and had acquired space underneath Victoria Station at Nottingham as a scenery store. Today, the only reminder of the Victoria Station is the impressive clock tower situated at the front of the shopping mall that replaced it. I have often wondered on my various engagements in Nottingham what stories that clock could tell about the people who used to meet under it. World War I curtailed Clements' activities but he was well prepared to carry on afterwards.

> ### JACK CLEMENTS' LOOSE GAGS
> **Feed:** Jack, how's your father?
> **Comic:** He's dead. Died with music on the brain. Someone hit him on the head with a trumpet.
>
> **Feed:** How long have you been on the dole?
> **Comic:** Since it started.
>
> **Feed:** What was your last job?
> **Comic:** I was on the railways.
> **Feed:** What doing?
> **Comic:** I was opening carriage doors.
> **Feed:** What for?
> **Comic:** To see if they were shut.

In the Suffolk town of **Lowestoft**, the South Pier, built by the Great Eastern Railway Company, had a pavilion added in the late Victorian period. In the latter part of the 19th and early 20th century, this housed various concert parties, including one managed by West End musical comedy star Broughton Black, who was also known for similar activities in the Devon resort of Torquay. In 1912 Will Edwards presented his entertainers there, and after World War I Randall Jackson's company occupied the pavilion for a while.

The Sparrow's Nest Gardens opened in 1897 with performances by the 'Olympian Pierrots'. Paul Hill was the leading artiste in the troupe and in 1900 he joined forces with the experienced Wallis Arthur. They entered into a contract with Lowestoft Corporation to present concert parties at the 'Nest', the South Beach Concert Pavilion and the Olympian Gardens. As these were all tented pavilions it was an expensive undertaking. They had not only to provide the flooring but all the seating as well — and the South Beach Pavilion alone could accommodate 1,000 people. It was a big gamble, even before considering the artistes' wages.

In those early years of the 20th century, many famous concert parties appeared at the Sparrow's Nest — Wilson James's 'Gaieties', the 'Lieutenants', the 'Scarleteers' (no prizes for guessing what colour they were dressed in!), the 'Olympian Entertainers' and the 'Tatlers', to name a few. In 1913 Lowestoft Corporation built the 1,100-seat Grand Concert Pavilion on the site of the old tented 'Nest', and one of Wilson James's companies, 'The Euterpeans', played there for the opening summer season in July of that year. The number of top-flight artistes who appeared at the Sparrow's Nest until its final demise in 1986 is like reading a 'Who's Who' of show business. We'll come back to some of those balmy days later.

One of the most exciting stories of a seaside venue began at **Clacton** on the Essex coast just before the turn of the century and was the foundation of a very successful entertainment that is still running now, and I'm sure will continue well into the 21st century.

Bert Graham arrived in Clacton as a comparative newcomer to entertainment, although he had been an amateur for a few years. There were already one or two alfresco pitches in the area with minstrel troupes. Graham wanted to start a concert party too, but his was to be slightly different; his small troupe would appear in evening dress at all times. He called his party the 'London Concert

Stanley Holloway — from Clacton to Hollywood!

Company' and performed alfresco during the day and by candlelight at night. Soon they made their mark in the town, becoming known as Graham and Russell's Concert Party, as Russell had been one of his original troupe. They moved to various venues in Clacton, at the turn of the century taking an open stage with a canvas covering in the West Cliff Gardens, the eventual site of one of today's great success stories.

Graham certainly knew how to pick his performers. One of them would become a well-known stage and film star here and in America: Stanley Holloway. Those who have seen the stage and film versions of *My Fair Lady* will remember his performance as Eliza Doolittle's dad, and his many Ealing film comedies of the 1950s. Holloway said his early experiences in concert parties were instrumental in his eventual success in films and musicals.

It was not just the east and west coasts of Britain that saw a growth of seaside entertainment in the Edwardian era. The sunny south coast would also become a happy hunting ground for many troupes. **Eastbourne**, in Sussex, owes a tremendous debt to the then Duke of Devonshire for its clean, colourful and attractive appearance, particularly the delightful Grand Parade with its outstanding floral display.

The Duke, who owned most of the land in Eastbourne, put in place certain covenants regarding the type of buildings that were to be erected on the sea front and elsewhere, and this helped to create the pleasant town which is so attractive today to residents and visitors alike.

There had been an appreciation for good music in Eastbourne well before the beginning of this century and many different bands played regularly on the bandstand at the shore end of the pier. Although the good folk of Eastbourne liked their music, it was to be a case of 'never on a Sunday' and even the Salvation Army fell foul of the local population who objected to their tambourines and drums and being saved from damnation. An Act of

Above: Graham and Bentley's company — Stanley Holloway, best-remembered for his brilliant role in the film version of *My Fair Lady*.

Left: Clacton-on-Sea's pier

'Mind your bloomers don't get wet, dear.'

PADDLERS, EASTBOURNE

Parliament curtailed their activities in the town on Sundays at least. As far as houses of entertainment were concerned, the town had them in a number of various forms. The first theatre was in South Street and presented mostly Victorian melodrama. The building lasted until 1882 when it was pulled down.

The Royal Hippodrome and Opera House in Seaside Road was built in 1883 and still stands today under the title of the Royal Hippodrome. What a lovely theatre it is. It has been threatened with closure once or twice in the past and what a disaster that would have been. Today it is mainly used for the presentation of light entertainment shows and concerts.

The Devonshire Park Theatre, built on the corner of Compton Street and Hardwick Road and within the boundaries of Devonshire Park itself, opened in June 1884. It was practically next door to the Winter Gardens, a large conservatory-type building which had opened a little while before. The Devonshire Park immediately

became a major touring date, with the company from the Garrick Theatre performing as a curtain-raiser to the new building and, at the turn of the century, direct from the Shaftesbury Theatre in London, the American Company in *The Belle of New York*. It is still a popular touring date today and also houses resident summer seasons of West End plays and artistes. It is also used by the local amateur operatic and dramatic companies. Today all the earlier venues in Eastbourne have been dwarfed by the Congress Theatre, which opened in 1963.

Eastbourne Pier has also seen a wealth of live entertainment since it was opened in 1870 by Lord Cavendish. The bandstand at the shore end was removed and rebuilt on the middle of the pier before World War I and was used by touring minstrel shows and concert parties. Meanwhile, all band performances were moved to a bandstand on the Grand Parade, where it is still part of the resort's entertainment programme.

On the site of the old bandstand, now removed, a new and larger music pavilion was erected at the shore end of the pier. The first theatre at the pier head had been a modest wooden edifice, built in 1888, seating just 400 people. This was replaced at the turn of the century by a large the-

Detail of Eastbourne Pier.

atre complex seating 1,000 people. Tragically, it was destroyed by fire in 1970. It was, however, rebuilt and is now a 'Dixieland Showbar' and is used for cabaret performances. We will cover in depth the Eastbourne entertainment scene after World War I later on.

Bournemouth was a genteel resort, as so many others were, before and just after the turn of the century. It is difficult to imagine that it is not yet 200 years since it was just a gap in the cliffs at the mouth of the River Bourne used mainly by 17th century smugglers. Its growth into the major resort it is now is due originally to two 19th century families, the Tregonwells and that of Sir George Tapps. Captain and Henrietta Tregonwell, who built themselves a house on the site of the present Royal Exeter Hotel, felt that the sea water around Bournemouth was health-giving and had special healing qualities.

In the early 1900s some visiting troupes of pierrots performed on the beach, including Will Catlin's parties. There were strict council regulations regarding the touring companies and the sort of entertainment provided.

But it was after World War I that Bournemouth really started to emerge as a venue for large concert parties. Visitors using the romantic Somerset and Dorset Railway including its famous 'Pines Express' (alas no longer in existence) from the Midlands and elsewhere to Bournemouth West Station, certainly took to the place in large numbers. The tradition has been maintained and put the busy and flourishing town in the forefront of seaside entertainment.

There is no doubt that Will Catlin had shown a distinctive flair as far as pierrot entertainment in Scarborough was concerned. But by the early 1900s he had also started to think of the future. By 1907 he had moved his entertainers off the beach and built a wooden

Left: Eastbourne Pier; note the original central location of the pavilion.

Below: The 'Gay Cadets' at Bournemouth in 1914.

Three of Bournemouth's 'Gay Cadets'.

Catlin's Royal Pierrots.

Above: Will Catlin (standing) with his 'Royal Pierrots', at Scarborough in 1911. He was called the 'biggest provider of public entertainment in the land.'

pavilion which he called 'Arcadia'. He very soon decided to build a more permanent and larger home for entertainment, seating up to 3,000 people and retaining the name Arcadia. A couple of years later he built the Arcadia Restaurant adjoining the theatre. In 1912, on the site of the Arcadia, he built the Futurist Cinema, the first super-cinema of its kind. This was to become the venue for the stage debut of tremendously successful television shows such as the 'Black and White Minstrels'.

In 1914 Catlin built the first holiday camp in this country, Kingscliffe, with accommodation for 1,000 people. *The Scarborough Evening News* wrote at the time, 'Catlin is the biggest provider of public entertainment in the land.' And he hadn't finished then. Later he moved to Llandudno which he not only made his new home, but ventured into further entertainment activities which we will discover later.

The pierrot companies on the sands around our coast laid the foundations for all future seaside entertainment. But they sometimes went through great hardships and inclement weather — gales and swirling sand and rain. In a heavy rainstorm the audience could vanish quite quickly taking shelter under the pier or the promenade wall. The pierrots could not run across the sands for shelter in their flimsy costumes so they would huddle together on their little platform, as if in a rugby scrum, to stop their make-up from running. If the weather looked as if it were going to be bad for some time, they would put up little notices near their pitches announcing 'If wet under the pier.' In later years, the notice would read, 'If wet in the Town Hall', or, as happened on occasions in Brighton, 'If wet in the Public Convenience': it must have been a very large one.'

'Your Country Needs You'

'Your country needs you' was the best known poster at the start of World War I, in August 1914. It asked all young men to volunteer for the armed services — and they did so in their droves over the next four years both from duty and under the pressure of their peers. This left the entertainment business at the seaside and elsewhere with the middle-aged and elderly for concert party companies.

Tradition had it that 'the show must go on', and some proprietors did indeed cope, keeping things going until the armistice in November 1918. This was four years later than expected: everyone said, 'It will all be over by Christmas'. (Where have we heard that before!)

Of course it wasn't, but apart from Scarborough, and other parts of the east coast that were shelled by the German Navy, there was some entertainment to be had for those at the seaside, such as at Morecambe, where the 'Seven Lancashire Lasses' and Ernest Binns and his 'Wavelets' carried on, as did Fred Clements at Skegness. Some of the west coast and southern resorts carried on as best they could, and other troupes came inland, where a profitable business developed.

A few concert parties went over to France to entertain the troops fighting there, enduring and sharing the hardships and dangers. One of the first to do this was Leslie Fuller, who named his troupe the 'Ped'lers' after the many dispatch riders who were given bicycles (hence the name)

when motor-bikes were in short supply! Fuller created his party to entertain service units in Britain, while they were waiting to go to France, and also for those who returned on leave or, more often, wounded and sick.

After the war the pierrot and concert party proprietors took over various venues in the cities at the end of their summer seasons. Leslie Fuller went to Margate where he became very popular. He also went into films in this country, and made a name for himself as a very creditable actor. To illustrate how popular he was in the Thanet area, there is a true story told about a film being made there starring George Arliss, a really famous screen idol in the 1920s and 1930s, especially in America.

Arliss was English, and the film required some shots of the exterior of an English mansion. The director saw the perfect house and went up to the front door, and enquired of the butler, who answered his ring, if his master would allow them to take some shots of the exterior of house.

Below: A pierrot troupe somewhere in France during World War I. The best-known of the hardy troupers who went over the Channel to entertain the troops was Leslie Fuller who named his troupe the 'Ped'lers', after the despatch riders.

Percy Merriman, who ran the 'Roosters'.

The butler replied that his master would not allow anyone to trespass on his land and shut the door.

Arliss heard about this and said to the director, 'Leave this to me. When he realises who I am, and that this is not some kind of joke I'm sure he'll agree to our request."

Arliss knocked on the door and repeated the request.

The butler was not to be moved, so Arliss now desperate said, 'Well at least let me have a word with your master, do you know who I am? I'm George Arliss."

The butler replied, 'I don't care if you're Leslie Fuller, buzz off!'

Fuller had definitely made his mark on Margate and Thanet audiences!

Percy Merriman also started a concert party during that war, naming his company the 'Roosters' and forming the troupe when he was serving in Salonika in Greece. After the war, Merriman decided to carry on in the entertainment business and formed the peacetime 'Roosters', who played seaside dates. A little later, the company did several radio broadcasts and some gramophone recordings on 78 discs.

Merriman wrote most of the material for his shows, and included some by those amazingly prolific writers of the interwar period, Wilcock and Rutherford. One particular song that I know a little about, and performed by the 'Roosters' was a Weston and Lee song 'Riding in a Railway Carriage.' They performed this with all the actions and noises of a train in motion. Part of it went something like this

> Riding in a railway carriage,
> Listen to the rhythm of the wheels,
> Throbbing, palpitating rhythm,
> Ev'ry one is tapping with their heels.
> 20 . . . 40 . . . 60 . . . 80 . . . miles,
> We rush along, rhythm, rhythm, rhythm,
> Rhythm, rhythm, rhythm at the wheels
> Riding in a railway carriage
> Riding to the rhythm of the wheels.

Top Right: The 'Roosters' concert party. Cousins Kenneth (bottom left) and George (top right) Western would go on to form the 'Western Brothers' double act.

Far Right, Top and Bottom: Fred Clements' entertainers at Skegness in 1915 (above) and 1916.

Right: 'Cardow's Cadets', another wartime troupe.

Concert party headgear 1915 style.

'Watch out for the Kaiser, lads.'

When the 'Roosters' disbanded, Merriman showed he was multi-talented, taking up one of his hobbies. He was a great authority on London and became a guide taking parties round the capital. He was also an admirer and authority on Charles Dickens, and performed a one-man show about the great Victorian writer.

I met his son, Eric, in the late 1950s when I joined the cast of radio's *Beyond Our Ken*, written by him. This was the start of my moving into the great and glorious age of British radio comedy. Eric has continued to write for many of our top-flight artistes, and now his son Andy has moved into writing for radio and has just published his first book which promises to be a big success — so three generations of Merrimans have been writing for the best part of 85 years.

Three more wartime troupes:

Right: Catlin's Great Yarmouth company, 1915.

Below Right: Carlton Fredericks' 'Les Vivandiéres' [sic] of 1917, seen at Weston-super-Mare.

Below: George Christian's 'royal Scarlet Pierrots', New Brighton, 1915.

CARLTON FREDRICKS

LES VIVANDIÈRES

Southsea South Parade Pier burning on 19 July 1904.

Above: The 'Quaints' programme for Saturday, 2 August 1913, South Parade Pier Theatre, Southsea.

Right: Southsea Parade and pier before World War I. The early piers proved to be combustible in the extreme, one reason being the amount of wood used in their construction. Southsea had a number of fires — as can be seen from the photograph at the top of the page.

The 'Olympians', a concert party to be found at the pier, Eastbourne, in 1914.

Left: Eastbourne Pier in the early 1900s.

Below Left: De la Warr Parade, Bexhill-on-Sea in the early years of this century.

Bottom Left: Watching the pierrots on the sands at Bognor Regis.

Pleasure Gardens Theatre, Folkestone.

Right: Worthing Pier opened in 1862 and in 1889 a pavilion was built at the pier-head. This Southern Pavilion, as it was known, was left isolated on Easter Monday 1913 when the middle and shore end succumbed to a gale. It reopened in 1914, and a new shore-end pavilion opened in 1926. The old Southern Pavilion was destroyed by fire in 1933, but replaced in 1935.

Below Right: Weymouth in Dorset has beautiful golden sands and a splendid promenade overlooked by a delightful terrace of small Georgian houses . Well before the turn of the century the sands were a haven for many different types of performer: Punch and Judy, solo banjoists, acrobats and, of course, the pierrots. Alexandra Gardens bandstand was later converted into a theatre, without losing its original design. Very much later prominent artistes did seasons there, with shows presented by Mr 'Show Business' himself Bernard (later Lord) Delfont. Weymouth has a fairly new pavilion at the end of the promenade which has a well furnished theatre and restaurant. Not far away is the port for ferry services to the Channel Islands.

Detail of the Victoria Pier, Blackpool.

Central Pier From the Entrance Blackpool

Left: Central Pier, Blackpool thronged with visitors. This postcard was from a Scottish visitor who extolled the pleasures of Lancashire in 1907.

Below: Swanage, on the Isle of Purbeck in Dorset, just down from Corfe Castle and the sandy beach at Studland, has been a holiday resort for many years. This view of the pier is dated 1910.

30479. SWANAGE PIER.

Above and Right:
Southport Pier opened in 1860, and waiting and refreshment rooms for steamer passengers were added two years later. Although there were visits by troupes of pierrots and concert parties to the town, there is no record of any taking place on the pier, or facilities for such. A unique baggage line was an early feature, and this was later upgraded to a passenger-carrying cable-operated tramway, which was electrified in 1905. Storm damage in 1933 and a fire in 1957 reduced its length, but it is still the second longest in Britain. At the shore end, the pier runs over a lake, a miniature golf course and a road, and there are amusements at the entrance. The tramway, now diesel-operated, takes passengers to the pier head, where there is a cafe and bar, a shop and amusement arcade. the photograph above shows aerial flight and water-chute in 1906.

Ladies taking sun at Scarborough around 1910.

Above Left: Will Catlin's 'Royal Pierrots' as seen in Whitley Bay, Newcastle, in 1907.

Above: Fred Pullan's 'Yorkshire Pierrots'. The troupe leader is seated.

Left: South Bay, Scarborough, c. 1905 — the year that the North Pier, built in 1869, was destroyed in a violent storm. Never a commercial success, it was not replaced.

Fred Pullan's 'Yorkshire Pierrots'.

Right: George Royle's 'Will o' the Wisps', Scarborough.

Below: Pierrots on the beach at Scarborough.

Far Right: Cover of an early Bridlington New Spa programme, showing views of the seafront.

THE WILL-O-THE-WISPS, THE SPA, SCARBORO'.

The beach at Bridlington.

BRIDLINGTON NEW SPA.
PROGRAMME.

IN THE BANDSQUARE.

FIREWORKS ON THE SPA.

The Spa.

The Pier Pavilion, Cleethorpes.

Right: Filey, near Scarborough, is another of the great east coast resorts. Here an early picture of pierrots playing to good crowd on the sands — how seaside entertainment started.

Below Right: The pier at Walton-on-the-Naze from a postcard sent in 1905.

Bottom Right: Postcard showing the beach at Southwold with a cross marking the house in which the sender was staying in the summer of 1906.

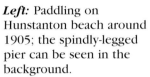

The old jetty at Great Yarmouth on a postcard sent in 1911.

Left: Paddling on Hunstanton beach around 1905; the spindly-legged pier can be seen in the background.

Below Left: The West Beach at Clacton-on-Sea with a good crowd watching the 'Pierrotts' — as this 1905 postcard would have them. Note the line of bathing carriages along the seafront and the retouched name 'Batty Photographer' centre right — I wonder whether this is advertising or early product placement?

Bottom Left: Mr Randall Jackson's Concert Party looks very smart for the 1907 season. Mr Jackson is the man at the extreme right of the photograph.

The Golden Years of Concert Party

Seaside entertainment between the wars

After four long years of war the public wanted entertainment and flocked to the seaside. There the challenge of providing what the customers wanted was taken up by the surviving impresarios.

Thanet had many concert party troupes in the area in the 1920s and 1930s: Ramsgate, Westgate and, particularly, Margate were popular. The latter boasted a number of splendid venues such as the Winter Garden and, not too far away on the lawns at Cliftonville, the Oval. With deckchair seating for 2,000 people, the Oval was a huge attraction for visitors and residents alike. In the mid-1920s Fred Wildon's 'Entertainers' were there with a cast that included a small, bespectacled Liverpudlian who would be a major force in the British entertainment industry for the next 60 years. His name? — today it's very familiar: Arthur Askey.

Askey stayed with Fred Wildon for two or three years before moving on to Shanklin on the Isle of Wight where again he was a huge success. He had made a big impact on the Margate audience — twice daily, afternoon and evening, at the open-air Oval venue without a microphone in sight. I think this is where the little man began putting funny movements to his comedy songs — if the audience missed a line at least they could laugh at his balletic actions.

Another important local venue was Margate Pier — although it was actually called Margate Jetty because it had been built with the Thames steamer trade in mind. In 1824 the Jarvis Landing Stage, a wooden structure, was erected but it was only used at low tide. In 1851 it was damaged by a storm, and so a new, more permanent structure was proposed. Eugenius Birch designed his first iron pier which was completed in 1857; soon afterwards a pier head and pavilion were added. It was damaged in 1877 by a drifting vessel, and more additions were made in 1893 and 1900.

Right: The Thanet area, which includes Margate, Broadstairs, Ramsgate and Westgate, was involved in pierrot and concert party entertainment from before the beginning of this century and after. Margate (seen here) was the centre. The air in the resort was apparently very good for those with respiratory problems — my mother used to say it had been beneficial to my father, who suffered from asthma. The bay was always very popular with visitors particularly from London from where regular steam ship services operated in the summer.

Far Right: Fred Wildon's 'Entertainers' were popular players during the 1920s at the Oval in Margate. Note Arthur Askey's involvement as indicated by his credits.

The Oval, Margate.

Arthur Askey at Shanklin.

Fred Wildon's Entertainers

....

OVAL - 3 p.m.

(If Wet, in Winter Gardens)

THURSDAY, JUNE 20th

....

1	" Smile "	*Wilcock*
	THE COMPANY	
2	" The Rain came pouring down " ...	*Arthur*
	THE COMPANY	
3	" A Song for Everyone "	*Wilcock*
	THE COMPANY	
4	" Nothing at all "	*Wilcock*
	MESSRS. ARTHUR ASKEY & GEOFFREY DUPREE	
5	" The Fishermen of England " ...	*Phillips*
	MR. LESLIE JONES	
6	" Shopping "	*arr G.D.*
	MR. GEOFFREY DUPREE	
7	" Awkward "	*Elliott*
	THE COMPANY	
8	" A Birthday "	*Woodman*
	MISS LILIAN MYERS	
9	" Father's Nose "	*Low*
	MR. ARTHUR ASKEY	
10	" Maiden in Grey "	*Barnicott*
	MISS LILIAN MYERS & MR. LESLIE JONES	
11	" I like Scented Soap "	*Weston*
	MISS DORIS LEE	
12	FRED WILDON in Musical Humour	
13	" The Music Stores "	*Beechcroft*
	THE COMPANY	

At the Piano ... MR. CYRIL WELLER

" GOD SAVE THE KING "

Fred Wildon's Entertainers

....

OVAL - 8 p.m.

WEDNESDAY, JUNE 19th

....

1	" Smile "	*Wilcock*
	THE COMPANY	
2	" A Jolly Day "	*Sutton*
	THE COMPANY	
3	" Oh, our Darling "	*Wilcock*
	THE COMPANY	
4	" The Death of D-O-R-A "	*Wood*
	MESSRS. ASKEY, DUPREE & WILDON	
5	" Days of Delight "	*Elliott*
	MR. LESLIE JONES	
6	" Stay out of the South "	*M.S.*
	MISS DORIS LEE	
7	" Don't you believe it "	*Sutton*
	THE COMPANY	
8	" Cherry Ripe " ... *arr Liza Lehmann*	
	MISS LILIAN MYERS	
9	" Ferdinand "	*arr G.D.*
	MR. GEOFFREY DUPREE	
10	" Love's Sentry " (Madame Pompadour) ...	
	MISS LILIAN MYERS & MR. LESLIE JONES	
11	' I pulled myself together "	*A.A.*
	MR. ARTHUR ASKEY	
12	FRED WILDON in Musical Humour	
13	" A Judicial Mix-up "	*Askey*
	THE COMPANY	

At the Piano ... MR. CYRIL WELLER

" GOD SAVE THE KING "

The 'Follies' performed at Sandringham in the presence of Edward VII.

Comedian Leonard Henry did a season there in concert party in the late 1920s. Perhaps it was just as well that he went on to carve himself a good career in musical comedy and radio because the shows on Margate Pier did not do very well.

Successful acts in the Thanet area included Bobby Howes, the father of stage and screen beauty, Sally Ann Howes. He was successful in concert party in Cliftonville. 'Uncle Mac' and his troupe were also regulars. Year after year from the early 1900s up to 1939 Mac entertained holiday makers at Broadstairs. His afternoon performances always included a children's talent concert. You can't beat this sort of presentation to bring in the kiddies and adults, it always works. He was such a favourite at Broadstairs that his association with the resort is commemorated with a plaque in his honour.

Leslie Fuller (mentioned in Chapter 1) also appeared at Margate. He and his 'Ped'lers' arrived there just after World War I. He was offered a tented pitch by landowner Jon Isles and was an immediate hit. By the mid-1920s he had moved to the new Clifton Concert Hall, (later renamed the Lido Theatre). Ethel Renwell and Gracie West were in his company and they went on to big successes in the halls and on radio in the 1940s and 1950s. The 'Ped'lers' had some marvellous sketches which they embellished with their own style of comedy.

In the 1930s Leslie Fuller and John Isles decided to go into the film business. They entered into a distribution agreement with the then powerful Gaumont British Film Corporation. Fuller himself was to act in some of the films they made.

Above: Leslie Fuller was a great name in seaside entertainment in the first half of the 20th century.

Right: The souvenir programme for the opening of Will Bentley and Bert Graham's West Cliff Gardens Theatre.

Margate would go on to even greater heights as an entertainments centre after World War II.

Clacton, too, soon adjusted to the post-World War I period. Will Bentley and Bert Graham planned a new theatre in West Cliff Gardens, and the Kingsman's family acquired Clacton Pier.

Graham and Bentley had submitted plans to construct a proper building on the site of the open-air stage in the gardens when the war finished. The scheme was eventually realised, and the West Cliff Gardens Theatre opened in May 1928. Their successes continued in the new theatre into the mid-1930s, until Bentley decided that his other business, an oyster bar in Piccadilly, London, demanded more of his attention. He and his partner sold the theatre to Will Hammer. They left behind a solid reputation and had encouraged several budding radio and theatre stars such as Ernie Leno, son of the great Dan Leno, the Western Brothers, Kenneth and George, Norman Long and Stanley Holloway.

Will Hammer already owned other theatres around the coast and, under his real name of William Hinds, a variety of other concerns — jewellery shops, hairdressing salons and a theatrical agency. He was also a comedian and liked to appear in small parts in his own shows, which he presented in association with band leader, Jack Payne who was already established on radio. It was Hammer who gave a young Frankie Howerd his early start in the business.

Hammer's ambition was to be a big film magnate and he soon formed a film company. In the 1950s, Hammer Film Productions Ltd. produced versions of radio hits like *Dick Barton, Special Agent, The Man in Black* and *Dracula*. Will realised there was money in horror and so the 'Hammer House of Horror' started.

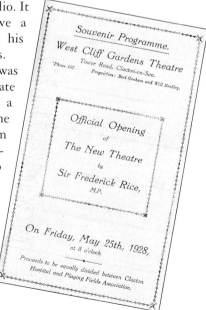

Willie Cave's 'Revels', Bournemouth 1932.

These films — such as *The Fall of the House of Usher* and *The Pit and the Pendulum* — have featured many great stars over the years, perhaps the best known being Vincent Price and the late Peter Cushing.

After Will Hammer died in 1957 the West Cliff Theatre had a chequered career. At one point it was suggested it should be demolished, as it needed a great deal of money spent on it. It was eventually saved, but only just, when it was purchased by Clacton District Council. In 1960 it reopened with repertory seasons, which did very well for several years and included West End stars like Bill Treacher, who appeared for some time in the popular BBC soap *Eastenders*.

At the same time as Bentley and Graham planned their new West Cliff Gardens Theatre, the Kingsman family — who had acquired the Clacton Pier early in the 1920s — decided to build a new pavilion on it at the shore end. Entertainment continued at the pier head with the 'Ramblas' Company; their venue, an open-air pavilion built by Kingsman in 1932, was called the Jolly Roger Theatre. The 'Ramblas' concert party was very successful for over 30 years (with a break for World War II, when it was closed down) and was the jumping-off ground for many revue performers.

The new shore-end pavilion — named the Ocean Theatre — could hold over a thousand people, and after opening with a circus, started a long succession of large scale summer shows. These ran until 1932 when a member of the cast, Frank Adey, was asked to produce; from then on the 'Ocean Revue' went from strength to strength, well into the 1940s.

On the south coast, in **Bournemouth**, seaside entertainment in the 1920s and 1930s was predominately in the hands of Birchmore and Lynden's 'Gay Cadets', and Willie Cave's 'Revels'. Cave's pitch was on the sands under the cliff lift, not far from the pier. George Fairweather worked for Cave and remembers those times with great affection. George, now 88 and still as bright as a button, went on to join W. H. Lester's 'Companions' and Walter Paskin's 'Come to the Show' where, incidentally, he met his future wife.

George finished his professional career in 1950 in the 'Windmill Follies' at nearby Boscombe, he later established a hairdressing business in Bournemouth and was 'By Appointment' to every male performer visiting the town who wanted his hair cut.

The Winter Gardens was occupied by the renowned Bournemouth Municipal Orchestra, founded and conducted by Dan (later Sir Dan) Godfrey. The BMO became one of the best-known British orchestras. It was regularly heard on the wireless in the 1930s and was also involved in gramophone recordings. Bournemouth residents and visiting artistes have always been fond of good music and the BMO certainly provided it.

Above Right: The 'Gay Cadets', Bournemouth 1924.

Right: Willie Cave's 'Revels' in Bournemouth during the 1930s. Standing third from left is George Fairweather.

Blackpool's Central Pier in 1934.

Left: Bournemouth Pier in the 1920s.

Below Left: The Central Pier, Blackpool, presented Tom Vernon's 'Royal Follies' in 1934.

Below: Headliners in the 'Royal Follies' 1934 programme were Phil Strickland — 'Yorkshire has been responsible for many things, but none more quaint and comical than Phil Strickland' — and Florence Oldham — 'A famous Artiste, with a famous Lancashire name'.

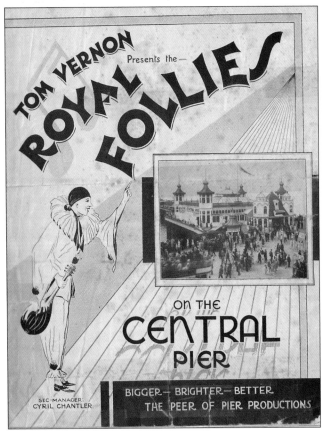

Jack Sheppard's 'Entertainers' in Brighton in the 1920s.

The resort's near neighbour to the east, **Boscombe**, saw many visiting concert party troupes, one of which featured a most eccentric gentleman by the name of Reuben More. At Boscombe, where business was not as good as elsewhere, Reuben would sit on the top deck of an open-topped bus, accompanied by his ventriloquist doll and talk to all the children riding on the bus through his doll. The children would talk back — to the doll — and this would encourage them to ask their parents to take them to see Reuben's concert party on the pier. Reuben was not only a ventriloquist but also a very passable comedian and writer of sketches and songs. His famous catch phrase was always the same: 'It's most eccentric!'

I was a resident in the **Brighton** area at one time, so I have a certain affection for the place and some knowledge of the history of the town's entertainment. There are also one or two family connections with both the piers. My father's cousin, playwright Roland Pertwee, took a lease on the Palace Pier theatre in the 1920s to try out his plays before taking them to London, and one of his sons, Jon Pertwee, was a member of a repertory company in the theatre on the West Pier, just before World War II.

It was about this time that band leader and showman Jack Hylton went to watch a comedian in Jimmy Hunter's Brighton Follies on the Palace Pier. Hylton immediately booked the comedian — it was Tommy Trinder — for one of his big touring shows, the beginning of a remarkable career that encompassed playing all the theatres in the United Kingdom, including the famous London Palladium. He later became known as the first host for television's much loved variety show — *Sunday Night at the London Palladium.*

The Aquarium, opposite the Palace Pier, was also a concert party venue — not inside the building with the fish, but on the roof. I can just imagine a soprano writing back home to her family saying, 'I'm performing on top of an aquarium'!

The wonderful Brighton Hippodrome, built by Frank Matcham on the site of an ice rink in Middle Street, was a magnificent theatre, all white marble, red plush, even a fountain — a huge attraction for patrons and artistes alike. In its early days, the Hippodrome housed a circus, but soon the circus gave way to music hall and variety weeks, revue, ballet and opera companies and full scale musicals. Laurence (later Lord) Olivier, made his first professional appearance playing in a sketch in revue at the Brighton Hippodrome in 1924, and on his first entrance tripped and fell flat on his face — not an auspicious start to a wonderful career.

Another famous name to be found in Brighton in the 1920s was Harry Sergeant. He arrived hoping to gain experience in summer shows, having played a couple of seasons before that in the north with Ernest Binn's 'Merry Arcadians', and Fred Roper and Bart Brady's 'Rogues'. However, it was Brighton that showed the way for Sergeant and later he made the town his home base.

Sergeant joined the 'Entertainers' run by Jack Sheppard, who had been in Brighton with his 'Highwaymen' since the latter part of World War I; he later changed the costumes of his company to modern dress, blazers and straw hats. Both his major pitches were outdoor: one, opposite Madeira Walk, was very near to the finishing line of the London-Brighton veteran car rally, and the other was opposite the Metropole Hotel near the West Pier.

Below: 'Saw a splendid company in *A Country Girl* on Saturday. Really as good as a London one.' Postcard of Brighton Palace Pier in the early 1900s.

Algy More (far left) in the 'Playtime Follies', Palace Pier,
St Leonards-on-Sea.

As in all alfresco shows, one of the company had to be a good 'bottler', going among the open air audience, watching from the promenade or other vantage point to coax them to part with a copper or two with the cry, 'Show your appreciation to the artistes. Thank you lady, thank you sir,' as the pennies dropped into the bottle. Harry Sergeant became a dab hand at this, and all the time he was learning his trade as a light comedian and passable dancer.

The girl he was to later marry was also in the show. She was a good critic and knew that Sergeant was ambitious to get on. She advised him to spread his wings and go out in the wider field of music hall and variety. This he did, and his wife also suggested a change of name — something catchy and easy to remember. After some discussion she said, 'How about Max Miller?' How that name came to mind we shall never know, but from that day on Max Miller conquered the world of music hall and variety as no one had done before.

From the 1930s to the 1950s he was top of the bill at theatres throughout the land, broadcasting regularly, and even recording some of his popular and saucy songs. The *London Evening News* said, 'Max Miller is the pure gold of the Music Hall.' He became a legend in the theatre and was, incidentally, the inspiration for John Osborne's character 'Archie Rice' in the play *The Entertainer*, which was made into a film starring Laurence Olivier.

Brighton's West Pier was popular right from the word go; in fact, in the mid-1870s some 600,000 promenaders disported themselves on what, at that time, was considered to be the finest pier in the British Isles. It was always thought by the local population that this area, adjacent to Hove (pronounced 'Hoove' in earlier days), was a cut above the rest, with its Regency terraces and sweeping lawns. The audience's fondness for music of the more sedate or classical kind was catered for in the magnificent glass pavilion with its potted palms and hot-house decor, built in 1916 halfway down the pier. This replaced the original bandstand and became a popular rendezvous.

The atmosphere on the West Pier changed somewhat after World War II with a more varied programme of entertainment, but its popularity never diminished.*

*If anyone wonders why I have not mentioned Brighton's lovely Theatre Royal, the Dome Concert Hall (with its popular organist for many years, Douglas Reeve), the Alhambra in the King's Road and the once-popular Grand Theatre: there's just not enough space!

There had been many Pierrot shows in **Hastings** before World War I, some of them playing on the Pier. However, it was in the 1920s that the resort became known for larger concert parties and revue companies. This was a direct result of the building of the White Rock Pavilion opposite the pier, the new theatre opening in 1927 with a season of the 'Fol-de-Rols', who carried on there into the 1930s.

In 1938 the 'Fols' companies included several future stars. One, Jack Warner, was later to make his name in films and the long-running TV series *Dixon of Dock Green*. Another was the operatic tenor and concert artiste Walter Midgeley, whose two children, Marietta and Vernon, in turn also became singing stars in their own right with appearances on BBC Radio's *Friday Night is Music Night*.

That little man with the glasses and the big heart from the Oval, Margate, and Shanklin Theatre, Arthur Askey, was also in the company, along with Richard Murdoch. They had both just started their radio series *Band Waggon*, which catapulted them to fame for the next 50 years.

More 'Playtime Follies'.

WHITE ROCK PAVILION.

HASTINGS.
[J. NORMAN GRAY.
Entertainments Manager]

FOR TWO WEEKS ONLY !

Commencing MONDAY, SEPTEMBER 2nd.   Evenings at 8.
MATINEE: WEDNESDAYS at 3.

THE

FOL-DE-ROLS

(EASTBOURNE COMPANY)

Artistes:

THE WESTERN BROTHERS

(KENNETH and GEORGE)
THOSE RADIO CADS!

MADELINE GIBSON   FREDERIC GREGORY
SOUBRETTE.   BARITONE.
TERRY RENDLE and SYLVIA NICHOLLS
SPECIALITY DANCERS.
EDITH PRICE   VERA FLORENCE
COMEDIENNE.   SOPRANO.
JOAN GILBEY FAY COLE
IN MINIATURE BALLETS AND ENSEMBLES.
ALMA MACKAY
ACROBATIC DANCER.
THE FOL-DE-ROLS ORCHESTRA
AND

MARRIOTT EDGAR

COMEDIAN.

CHANGE OF PROGRAMME MONDAY AND THURSDAY.

MONDAY, SEPT. 16th—Return of the Hastings Company of

THE FOL-DE-ROLS

for LAST TWO WEEKS of the Season, Farewell Performance 30th Sept.

ADMISSION : Reserved, 3/6 and 2/6 ; Unreserved, 1/10, 1/3 and 9d.
Booking Office Open: Weekdays, 10.30 a.m. to 8.30 p.m.; Sundays, 3 p.m. to 5 p.m.   Telephone 1840.
Phone 2450.   P.T.O.

Hastings Printing Co., Portland Place and Tower Road.

During the 'Fol-de-Rols' seasons in the 1930s, one of the company members, Harry Hanson, decided to try his luck in management and took a lease on the Hastings Pier Theatre to run a repertory company. His new career in management soon took off and he continued to present his companies for many, many years all over England, not only at seaside resorts but also inland towns and cities.

Folkestone and **Hythe** had their fair share of visiting concert parties, some of them playing for just a week or two at the beginning of the season before taking up a summer residency at another resort. Folkestone had a pavilion very near the present harbour and also the new Cliff Hall which then catered for celebrity concerts and recitals. Nearby was the bandstand, staging military band concerts in the afternoons.

Far Left: Hastings 1935 — White Rock Pavilion, with the pier entrance in the foreground.

Left: Hastings and Eastbourne 'Fol-de-Rols' swap venues for two weeks in the 1930s.

Below: Folkestone Pier — alas, no more!

On the sands at Bognor in the 1930s.

Left: Bognor Pier showing the impressive theatre.

Below: 'Twinkle' — a 'super summer show' for 1931.

Right: Miss Noreena Feist danced with a 'certain clever company calling themselves the "Bunch of Keys"' in Devonshire Park, Eastbourne.

Some way off the front there was the Pleasure Gardens Theatre, where not only concert parties played but also some of the larger touring companies, even sometimes full West End musicals, complete with orchestras.

Bognor Regis, with its early Victorian architecture on the promenade and in Steyne Square, was a very popular resort from the 19th century, and its sunny beaches were enough to provide the early entertainment. There was Fred White's 'White Coons' company on the sands and later on the lawns, and Uncle George and his 'Thespians' opposite the Steyne. Later, Wallis Arthur (a very good concert party manager) appeared regularly at Bognor and his company included Clarkson Rose, who learned a lot from Arthur during his time there. 'Clarkie' went on to devise and produce his own show, 'Twinkle', at a later date.

While a certain Clifford Gray appeared in the 'Drolls', he found fame and fortune when he wrote *If You Were The Only Girl In The World*, with which George Robey and Violet Lorraine set London alight in *The Bing Boys* (the show every Tommy home from France wanted to see). Concert parties also featured on the pier and, in the theatre at the shore end, seasons of repertory were popular. Much later there were variety shows.

St Leonards in Sussex, the slightly quieter neighbour of Hastings, once had a pier with a pavilion, which housed various entertainments and a resident orchestra. However, they left in the very early 1920s and from then on business in the pavilion declined and the pier changed hands. There was a pierrot pitch on the pier, one of them being the 'Playtime Follies', which included Algy More, the son of eccentric Reuben More (a name that has cropped up in this book

BESIDE THE SEASIDE

From the 'Fol-de-Rols' seaside summer show programme, Eastbourne during the 1930s.

more than once). The pierrot pitch on the pier later became a swimming pool, which reminds me of a strange experience that happened to me and my old mate from *Dad's Army*, Clive Dunn. About 20 years ago, we were booked to do a week's variety at the Nell Gwynne Theatre in Hereford. There was a bar, a cafeteria and dressing rooms, but the swimming pool was where we had to play — with us in the deep end, the audience in the shallow end and in chairs around the outside of the pool. Clive and I coped with it and had quite an enjoyable week, particularly in the hotel where we stayed with the small band. In the end, the pier at St Leonards was demolished in 1951.

A little further round the coast from St Leonards lies **Bexhill-on-Sea**, a genteel resort with a pleasant promenade, delightfully designed houses and a long front leading to Cooden Bay, some way away. There was a large entertainment centre, the Kursaal, which housed various attractions, including touring pierrot troupes and concert parties. In 1936 a large all-purpose concert hall with various amenities was opened — the De La Warr Pavilion. It was named after Earl de la Warr, a leading light in the area's development. Many of the grand houses in Bexhill are now divided into flats or have become hotels, but Bexhill still has a comfortable feeling about it.

Worthing has seen a lot of entertainment in its time, mostly on the pier. In its early days, it was also a rather genteel resort, in some contrast to its near neighbour, the busier and more flamboyant Brighton. Worthing still retains that image in some ways, as it has a fairly large population of retired people who continue the resort's liking for good music. The first pavilion was built in 1888 at the seaward end of the mid-19th century pier. The pier was not only used for promenading by the ladies in their fine dresses and the gentlemen in blazers and boaters, but it was also the embarkation point for the many popular steamer trips that plied up and down the coast. It was cut in half in the gales of 1913, but somehow the pavilion survived like an offshore island. Rebuilding was immediately put in hand and the pier reopened a year later.

In the mid-1920s a new pavilion was erected at the shore end and it played host to musical concerts and concert parties, one of which — the 'Moonlight Follies' — became very popular. In 1933 fire struck, and the seaward pavilion was destroyed. However, two years later the pier had been repaired and the new pavilion built, complete with a solarium fitted with special glass to attract the sun's rays, and a first floor balcony. The shore end

pavilion, meanwhile, continued with concerts, music recitals and concert parties. In 1940, a huge hole was blown in the middle of the pier to stop the Germans from using it as a landing point and the ARP used the pavilion for their various activities! I will return with some personal memories of Worthing in Chapter 3.

Probably the most significant event in **Eastbourne**'s pier entertainment after World War I took place in 1924, when two performers who had been in the 'Fol-de-Rols' at Scarborough, Felgate King and his wife Elsie Mayfair, came south and decided to form their own concert party company. They launched it in the newly-built music pavilion at the shore end of the pier.

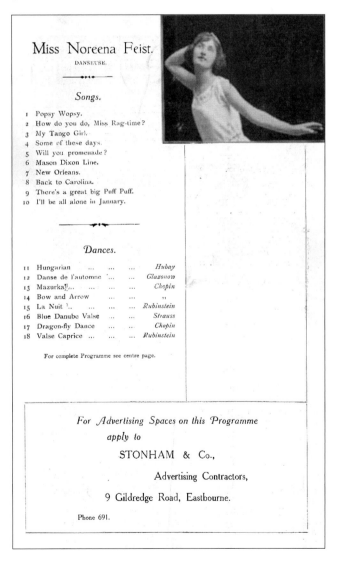

Miss Noreena Feist.
DANSEUSE.

Songs.

1 Popsy Wopsy.
2 How do you do, Miss Rag-time?
3 My Tango Girl.
4 Some of these days.
5 Will you promenade?
6 Mason Dixon Line.
7 New Orleans.
8 Back to Carolina.
9 There's a great big Puff Puff.
10 I'll be all alone in January.

Dances.

11	Hungarian				*Hubay*
12	Danse de l'automne				*Glazonow*
13	Mazurka				*Chopin*
14	Bow and Arrow				,,
15	La Nuit				*Rubinstein*
16	Blue Danube Valse				*Strauss*
17	Dragon-fly Dance				*Chopin*
18	Valse Caprice				*Rubinstein*

For complete Programme see centre page.

For *Advertising Spaces* on this *Programme*
apply to
STONHAM & Co.,
Advertising Contractors,
9 Gildredge Road, Eastbourne.
Phone 691.

51

Sandy Powell and his daughter in a 1930s film.

DEVONSHIRE PARK,
— EASTBOURNE. —
Manager and Secretary———EDGAR ALLAN BROWN.

: IN THE :
PAVILION

A

Vaudeville Season

— BY A —
CERTAIN CLEVER COMPANY
— CALLING THEMSELVES —

"The Bunch of Keys"

UNDER THE DIRECTION OF
— MR. ERNEST BUTCHER. —

Programme.

— PRICE ONE PENNY. —

The Felgate King Company became so popular that it stayed there until 1934. The couple had brought with them their young son, Peter, who had been born during one of their seasons at Scarborough — almost 'born in a trunk' as the saying goes. He spent his summer holidays at Eastbourne helping his parents and eventually made his first stage appearance with them.

In 1935 Clarkson Rose and Olive Fox took over the pavilion to present 'Twinkle'. Clarkson Rose, wily show-man that he was, brought young Peter into his company for that first season and advertised his name on the posters

as Felgate King Junior, thinking this would help him to establish 'Twinkle' and give his show an extra boost, his predecessors having been so successful.

Rex Newman, the 'Guv'nor' of the 'Fol-de-Rols', arranged for young Peter to go into a couple of other sea-side companies so that he could gain extra experience before taking his place in the 'Fols', which he did in 1939. His next 'engagement', like so many others of his genera-tion, was in France, and it proved to be not short of a few adventures.

After the war, now using his real name of Felgate, Peter was to re-establish himself not only with the 'Fols' but in the West End theatre too. The 'Fol-de-Rols' had a company at Hastings in 1938 and also at Eastbourne's Floral Hall in the Winter Gardens that year. The hugely popular 'Co-optimists' concert party had also played there earlier in the 1920s and they were to take their multi-tal-ented company, which included Stanley Holloway, to other resorts before their record-breaking season in London's West End.

Adjacent to the Winter Gardens was the Devonshire Park Theatre. This continued to fly the flag of straight theatre with visits by some popular West End stars, such as Phyllis Neilson Terry in *Trilby*, and a production of *Joan of Arc* with Francis L. Sullivan, who later featured in many British films. Robert Coote (destined to be the orig-inal Colonel Pickering in the Broadway production of *My Fair Lady*) appeared there in *The Farmer's Wife*, and George Robey, the 'Prime Minister of Mirth' as he was known, brought his popular show *Bits and Pieces* to the venue in the 1920s.

In the early 1930s Tom Arnold and the legendary C. B. Cochran presented their revue *One Damn Thing After Another*. Other stars to visit 'The Park', as it was affec-tionately known, were Jessica Tandy (*Driving Miss Daisy*), a young Rex Harrison playing such a minor role he didn't warrant a mention in the programme, and an equally young James Mason in *The Fanatics* who, fortunately, was acknowledged! Pantomime also flourished there under the banner of producer Murray King.

Towards the end of the 1930s the Devonshire Park took a big gamble with an ice show presented by Tom Arnold. The whole stage was frozen solid with ice and it all worked very well, thus proving that giving the audi-ence something different is always an attraction!

One of the last plays to be seen at 'The Park' just before World War II was J. B. Priestley's *When We Are*

Clarkson Rose.

Married, which included an unforgettable performance by that wonderful comedian Robb Wilton.

From time to time the theatre underwent considerable and necessary repairs, resulting in the resident repertory companies moving over to the Royal Hippodrome in Seaside Road as a temporary home. The Hippodrome in the late 1920s played host to an assortment of attractions. One notable revue, entitled *Here's To You*, starred Bud Flanagan and Chesney Allen, the fondly remembered stars of the later 'Crazy Gang', and a young comedian polishing his craft, later to take London by storm in the 1940s and 1950s — the great Sid Field.

In 1928, at the Winter Garden Theatre, there was an appearance by the renowned Scottish comedian, Sir Harry Lauder, and in the same year Sir Edward Elgar conducted his own work *The Dream of Gerontius*. The following year the American singer, Paul Robeson, played to an absolutely packed house, standing room only. In 1935, on the occasion of George V and Queen Mary's Silver Jubilee, the Winter Gardens hosted a grand ball, with music provided by Roy Fox and his Band.

The lawns at **Southsea**, with wonderful views over the Solent and a backdrop of large and attractive Victorian houses, was an occasional venue for small pierrot troupes, while the large South Parade Pier Pavilion housed concert parties and, later, more sophisticated summer revues. Eccentric proprietor Reuben More had a concert party pitch very near Clarence Pier. Today, the hovercraft to the Isle of Wight operates from exactly the same spot.

One afternoon, in the middle of a matinee, Reuben's concert party pianist, Moses Mudd, jumped up suddenly from the piano and said in a loud voice, 'I've got the call, I must go.' With that he rushed out through the audience of the tented venue, across the lawns, and was never seen again. The first reaction of most people when he shouted, 'I've got the call,' was that he was going to the nearby toilets. His close associates soon realised that 'the call' had probably meant he was off to join the Salvation Army, something he had been talking about for a long time. As for Reuben More's reaction: well, anything unusual didn't make him angry so much as amused. All he said on Moses's exit was, 'Most eccentric, most eccentric.'

Just one of the eccentric things about Reuben himself was that, when he paid the members of his company, he would ask them to gather outside his lodgings, wherever they were playing, and he would drop the individual wage envelopes in a slipper from his bedroom window, one by one on the end of a large piece of string. I wish I had known Reuben and all his eccentricities. Luckily I got to know his son very well and he could make me roar

Left: The 'Bunch of Keys', Eastbourne, 1930s.

Below: Postcard of South Parade Pier, Southsea. On the back: 'Dear Mother,' writes son Douglas Taylor, 'the apples are 5d per pound. I am just going back to school.'

Reuben More and company at Ventnor.

THE PIER, VENTNOR.

with laughter with his anecdotes of the entertainment business.

Clarence Pier was destroyed during one of the World War II air raids on adjoining Portsmouth. It was rebuilt, but only on the shore foundations, and became what can only be described as a theme park with large fairground-type attractions, complete with fast food and ice cream parlours.

The **Isle of Wight** has a long tradition as a venue for the entertainment business. The Theatre Royal in Ryde, one of the major ports for passengers from the mainland, had a thriving business in the early 19th century. Actress Mrs Jordan, the mistress of William, Duke of Clarence (later King William IV), was in the Theatre Royal Company, as were Henry Irving and Ellen Terry at a later date. In 1922 that wonderful, slightly eccentric, racing gambler, Wilfred Hyde White (he of *My Fair Lady* fame) made his stage debut at the Royal in *Tons of Money*. The theatre is now no more; today a bank stands on the site.

There were touring and resident pierrot shows and concert parties in all parts of the island, and the old Gaiety Theatre at Freshwater was a particularly popular venue. Shanklin, Ventnor and Sandown piers were others where patrons spent many happy hours in the presence of seaside entertainers.

At Cowes, before the turn of the century, a pierrot party led by Francis Essex, performed near the yacht club and the Prince of Wales, later Edward VII, invited this troupe to give a performance in his presence. The prince was so impressed with it that he asked Essex whether one of his company could teach him to play the banjo. This was arranged and the Royal Seal was put on the troupe: from then on they were called Francis Essex's 'Royal Pierrots'. Much later in life, Essex, who incidentally had been the first to adopt the pierrot costume when he performed at Bray near Dublin, became a very distinguished song publisher as Essex Music in London.

In the very early 1920s that rascal Reuben More had concert parties at Ventnor and Ryde. In the Ventnor Company his principle comedian at one time was Bobby Dunn, the father of Clive Dunn. Once, when Reuben was producing a show in the pavilion at the Ryde pier-head

Elsie and Doris Waters.

and business was poor, he decided it was time for extreme measures to publicise the show and the pavilion.

He persuaded a man, for a few shillings, to 'accidentally on purpose' jump off the pier during a matinee performance of the show, and feign drowning; of course, More assured him he would immediately be rescued. The 'drowning' was to coincide with the show's singer giving his familiar rendition of *On With The Motley* in full Pagliacci regalia. At a given shout of 'man overboard', Reuben signalled to his singer to run off-stage, down through the audience and jump into the sea to save the drowning man. For this, the singer would get an extra week's wages.

The unfortunate thing was that nobody had told Reuben his singer was a non-swimmer, so he ended up having to be saved with the drowning man! The event was given full coverage in all the local newspapers, including the Portsmouth editions, and brought a lot of publicity for the show. As Reuben More would say, 'It turned the business.' Ryde Pier was demolished many years ago and it is now a car parking area.

Another very enthusiastic concert party proprietor was Powis Pinder. Pinder was originally at the Ryde Pier Pavilion but wanted to spread his wings, so he passed on the date to Clarkson Rose, who was in his first season in management with his 'Twinkle' Company. Pinder moved to Shanklin Pier but only for a short time, as the theatre was burned down. It was fairly quickly rebuilt to accom-

modate Terry Wood, who took a lease on the Shanklin Pier Theatre. One of the artistes in his company in the 1930s was comedian Tommy Trinder.

Pinder was an optimist and quickly decided to build his own theatre at Shanklin on the promenade. He bought some old seaplane sheds left over from World War I in Bembridge Harbour, and had them remodelled into a quite adequate theatre. It was put up on the site of an old

Left: Ventnor Pier, Isle of Wight.

Below: Clarkson Rose (centre back) and the first 'Twinkle' company. Olive Fox is in centre front. The company would celebrate its 25th anniversary in 1946.

Bottom: The esplanade and pier, Ryde, Isle of Wight.

Above: Tommy Handley who would go on to make it big in *ITMA*.

Albert Modley in character.

semi-open-air structure. I spent some happy hours with Pinder's son, Arthur, and his wife, some 20 years ago, and he told me an amusing story about his father at Shanklin. His show 'Sunshine' was in competition with Terry Wood's show on the pier and on some evenings Powis used to stand outside his theatre with a pair of binoculars trained on the pier box office, to see how many people were going in and whether it was more than were attending his theatre on the promenade. How anyone could 'count the house' (an old theatrical phrase) from that distance I have no idea!

In 1926, Arthur Askey arrived from the Oval at Margate to join Pinder's 'Sunshine' company for the next step on his journey to stardom. Askey was in Shanklin from 1926 to 1937, the year that radio's *Band Waggon* series catapulted him to success. During that time he made many friends and delighted thousands of theatre goers with his merry quips and comic songs, such as *The Bee*. He and his wife May had a lovely bubbly daughter called Anthea, who went to school in Shanklin while her parents were at the resort.

Some of the other members of the 'Sunshine' cast at Shanklin went on to have successful careers. Teddy Styles became a well known film actor, both here and in America; Bernard Lee also made it in films, particularly as 'M' in the James Bond films, and singers Ann

Zeigler and Webster Booth became very popular in concerts and on radio.

When World War II put a stop to seaside entertainment, Shanklin Theatre was used as a storage area for some of the famous PLUTO (pipeline under the ocean) accessories: so you could reasonably say that Pinder's Theatre played its part in winning the war as PLUTO conveyed much-needed oil to the French coast after the Normandy landings. At the end of the war the theatre was in such a bad state of repair that it was thought not worth renovating. However, some years later it was refurbished and it is now an amusement arcade.

Once the war was over (as we shall see in Chapter 3), the island again offered the best in entertainment, with many big stars being attracted to its various venues.

The small, attractive resort of **Teignmouth** on the Devon coast was merely a fishing village before the start of its redevelopment early in the 19th century. It is now a delightful small brother to nearby Torquay. There is a lovely view of it from Shaldon on the other side of the River Teign, the mouth of which can be crossed by a regular ferry service. Teignmouth still has port facilities which are used regularly for bringing in timber and transporting local clay.

Teignmouth has regular summer show entertainments at the small Carlton Theatre and also amateur repertory

Right: The sea front from the pier, Teignmouth, 1931

Above Right: 'On With The Show' at the North Pier, Blackpool, in the 1930s.

Detail from 'On with the Show' programme.

seasons. The pier was a much-used concert party venue, but today, what is left of the original structure contains only amusements, shops and fairground rides.

One summer in the 1920s, Leslie Henson, who later became a London musical comedy star, had his concert party on the pier. During the season he was presenting a new sketch which required a large bang in the middle of it. Henson was full of fun and always willing to experiment. He decided the best way to get the effect he wanted was to put a maroon in a dustbin. This was placed by the back of the stage entrance to the pavilion and, at the appropriate moment, it was fired. It worked brilliantly, but such was the force of the explosion that it blew the door off its hinges with a bang that could be heard for miles around. Within a few minutes the Teignmouth lifeboat put to sea searching for a boat in distress. I'll bet there were a few stories that night circulating round the local pubs!

There is a small, but very well put together, guide of the historic town from the tourist office; what's more it's free and well worth reading.

Newquay, on the rocky north Cornish coast with its magnificent scenery and miles of golden sands, is now famous for its wonderful surfing beaches. Back in the 1920s its fame was in a small theatre with a big reputation — the 'Cosy Nook' near the harbour. Foremost among the companies who entertained the well-heeled audiences, resplendent in evening dress straight from the dinner tables of the many opulent hotels in the area, was a show called 'Kabaret Kittens' run by the entertainer Ronald Frankau. He also had another company entitled the 'Blues'.

Among the 'Kittens' was a young conjuror called Naunton Wayne, who was destined for the London stage and films. Who can forget his performance in the original version of *The Lady Vanishes* when he and Basil Radford, played the two cricket-mad travellers Charters and Caldicot? Ronald was to become a very big name in radio in the 1930s and 1940s when he teamed up with Tommy Handley in various guises, such as Murgatroyd and Winterbottom and Colonel Curry and Major Rice.

For many years there were a number of people who had the faith and foresight to realise that **Blackpool**, with its surrounding beaches and attractive areas, was a resort that would appeal to a different type of holiday-maker, someone in fact looking for fun, excitement and good entertainment. One of the first to realise the potential was Thomas Sergenson, and in 1880, at the age of 27, he decided a raucous blend of comedy, popular music and melodrama could be made to pay where others had failed with a more sophisticated brand of entertainment.

After taking out short leases on various theatres he had made enough money to purchase a row of shops. His idea was to build a 'grand' theatre on the site. After much jealousy from other entertainment entrepreneurs in the town who tried to outmanoeuvre him, Sergenson finally got his way and the beautiful Grand Theatre was designed and built for him by the brilliant architect Frank Matcham.

Another young man who had his eye on Blackpool in the 1920s was Lawrence Wright, musician and song writer. Wright was born in Leicester, and after leaving school he joined a concert party where he played some of the instruments, including the piano, which he had mastered at a very early age. He started his musical career by

Albert Modley — 'On With The Show'.

selling sheet music from a stall in his home town, but the project nearly failed when, quite by chance, he heard a busker singing a song *Don't Go Down The Mine Daddy*, and bought it for a few shillings. With this, he made enough money to try his luck in London, but was determined not to spend any of his hard-earned cash on the fare to the capital, so he walked from Leicester to London! He found a job playing the piano demonstrating the copies of sheet music that were being sold from the publisher's offices in Denmark Street, just off Charing Cross Road, the centre of the music business and already nicknamed 'Tin Pan Alley'.

After service in World War I, he began writing his own songs under the name of Horatio Nicholls — Horatio, after the British naval hero, Nelson, and Nicholls after the American slang for one of the country's coins, a 'nickel'. He had almost immediate success, and two compositions in particular — *Among My Souvenirs* and *Toy Drum Major* — catapulted him to fame and fortune. He bought a Rolls-Royce with the profits and opened up other music stores in Llandudno, the Isle of Man and Blackpool, where he was to stay for the rest of his life.

Wright engaged Jack Hylton and his band at one point to fly round the Blackpool Tower and along the shore, playing one of his songs, *Me And Jane In A Plane*, as copies of the music were showered down on the amazed public who had gathered in their thousands for the event.

In 1924 Wright decided to go into summer season management on the North Pier. He titled his production 'On With The Show' and he stayed there for 32 consecutive years. There had been some very good pierrot troupes and concert parties on the piers in the 1920s and 1930s, but it was Lawrence Wright with his productions on the North Pier that started a new trend of not only engaging new talent but also established performers, and blending the two together with extremely successful results.

In Blackpool Wright was in competition with Bert Feldman's music shop. Bert, too, was a song plugger and stayed on in the resort after Wright retired, although it was the latter's flair for publicity combined with his musical talent that had really put him out in front. All the top names in show business sang his songs at one time or another, and for some in particular he wrote especially, and they became big hits.

In the period between the wars, there were some personalities that Blackpool quickly adopted as its own. George Formby was one of them. He was born in Wigan, one of seven children, but as his father was a well-known music hall performer, the family didn't exactly starve. George (who, incidentally, was born blind and didn't see until he was six months old) didn't enjoy his schooldays very much: his teacher said he couldn't do sums or read too well, so his father took him away from school and he became a stable boy in Ireland, where his father had a race horse. He became very good with horses and started training to be a jockey. However, the life was too hard for this very young lad and he ran away from Dublin and went back home. He arrived at the dock to catch the mail boat to Holyhead

'With My Little Stick of Blackpool Rock.'

but the barriers had just closed. He didn't know it at the time but he was the luckiest boy alive. It was wartime, and the boat he missed was torpedoed in the Irish Sea with the loss of 500 passengers and crew.

George eventually got back home and decided a little later to follow in his father's footsteps on the halls. His father died in 1921, and young George's first professional appearance was in that same year.

He married Beryl in 1924, the beginning of a partnership in which Beryl was to be a major player. They made Blackpool their home, and they had a succession of houses during the time they were there. When the new opera house was opened by Jessie Matthews in 1939 George played the first season with his show 'Turned Out Nice Again'.

George did practically everything in show business. A great stage personality, he is best-remembered for singing all those wonderful funny songs accompanying himself on his ukulele. His films broke box office records — in fact in the 1930s he was voted the most popular film actor in the county, well ahead of all the American stars.

During World War II, he was one of the first into France to entertain the British troops in 1939 and the beginning of 1940. He was very popular with the Royal Family and entertained them at Windsor during the war, singing the original lyrics of his saucy songs (some of which had been banned by the BBC) at the request of the king and queen. He came to London with the hit show 'Zip Goes A Million', not only as a top of the bill variety performer but also as a very good stage actor. George and Beryl died within a year of each other in the early 1960s.

I remember in 1938, when I was 12, buying all of George's 78rpm records on Regal Zonophone Red Label, and my very sophisticated Aunt Amy eventually became a fan of his after hearing them on her new radiogram.

Another of Blackpool's favourites — always referred to as Blackpool's adopted son — was the diminutive and very talented Jimmy Clitheroe. He was only 4ft 2in tall, and one might imagine his lack of height and round, boyish face would have restricted his progress as an entertainer: far from it — in fact they became his principal assets and trademark.

He was born in Clitheroe in Lancashire and at the age of 14 joined a troupe of juveniles, playing an accordion, an instrument his mother had taught him. The accordion was almost as big as little Jimmy! He first appeared in Blackpool in 1930 and was almost a regular entertainer

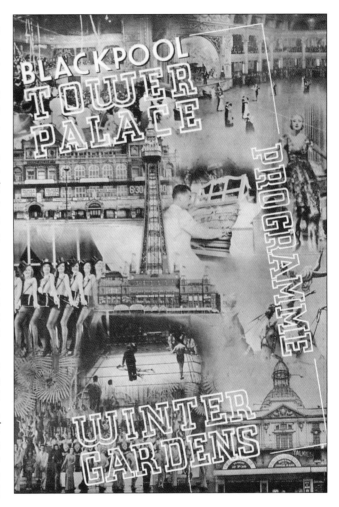

Above: Blackpool Tower & Winter Gardens programme — yours for the princely sum of 2d.

Left: Robert Donat, star of stage and screen, makes a personal appearance in Blackpool.

there until 1971 when he topped the bill at the North Pier, with Freddie and the Dreamers.

The 'Clitheroe Kid', as he was always called by his fellow artistes who all had a great respect and admiration for him, was also known to millions of radio listeners who tuned in to his record-breaking radio shows. They spanned 14 years, with peak-time audiences and a wonderful supporting cast of great performers. That show, *The Clitheroe Kid*, was heard all round the world, and is today

Victoria Pier, Blackpool (now the South Pier).

one of the most popular programmes in the BBC radio collection.

Some producers tried to exploit Jimmy's size as something freakish but he would have none of it. He was a good businessman as well as the ever-juvenile artiste and his fans would not have stood for it; they had too much respect for him, and he for them. Jimmy's ever helpful mother died in 1973 and Jimmy himself died at the age of 51, on the day of his mother's funeral.

Danish heart-throb, Carl Brisson, a boxer turned singer, played at the Grand Theatre in 1923 in a revival of *The Merry Widow* with the beautiful and talented Evelyn Laye. (To think I was to work with her 60 years later in a season at the Chichester Theatre!) Evelyn had a varied career and went on to star in this country and on Broadway in musical comedy. She also worked with the Crazy Gang at one time.

As for Carl Brisson, he loved Blackpool and the reception he got from the Grand Theatre audiences was tremendous. His son Freddie went to school in Blackpool while his father was there, and he, too, became involved in entertainment, as an executive in America where he married the wonderful stage and screen actress Rosalind Russell.

Gracie Fields was another huge favourite at the Grand Theatre from her earliest appearances in 1929. She received a huge welcome with packed houses in a production called *The Show's The Thing*. Blackpool was used as a location in her starring movie *Sing As We Go* in 1934. What a wow that was! I can remember in the mid-1930s walking along Erith High Street, near where we were living, and listening to the title song being played in Woolworths. People would join in as they walked by:

Sing as we go, and let the world go by
Singing a song we march along the highway.

It made you feel good, and that is what Gracie did throughout her long career. She brought the same sort of feeling to the troops she entertained on the battle-

fields during World War II. Sadly, her early personal life was not always happy, but few would have guessed as much from her cheery on-stage *joie de vivre*. She did find true happiness towards the end of her life with her beloved Boris, and her home in Capri. She was a wonderful entertainer and when audiences heard her signature tune — *Sally* — as she was about to walk on stage, the theatre erupted. Despite all the adulation she never forgot her roots in Rochdale and the town was later to honour their own 'Lancashire Lassie'.

In 1941 comedian Harry Korris wrote a radio script called *Happidrome* and the BBC decided to do it. This led to a four-year run with audiences as big as *Coronation Street* today. It ran for 200 performances until 1947.

Korris had first appeared in Blackpool in 1931 in Ernest Binn's Pierrot Company the 'Arcadian Follies'. He did many seasons in the resort, including nine successively at the South Pier. In the radio show he had an old friend, Robbie Vincent, playing a call boy called Enoch whose catchphrase — 'let me tell you' — was on everybody's lips at the time. So, too, was Korris's character Lovejoy, 'Ee, if ever a man suffered; take him away Ramsbottom', the latter played by Cecil Frederick. The show's signature tune, *We Three in Happidrome, Working for the BBC, Ramsbottom and Enoch and Me* was hummed and whistled everywhere. Korris went on to make a number of successful low budget films in the north, particularly with Frank Randle. He starred with that super musical comedy star, Pat Kirkwood, at the Grand and would have had his name in lights for the first time but because it was wartime no lights were allowed.

Wilkie Bard, originally a singer of peculiar songs such as *She Sells Sea Shells on the Sea Shore*, was one of the first comedians to use his own stooges placed in the audience for crosstalk repartee. He almost invented the double act on stage, using walk-on artistes and others who constantly interrupted him in the middle of his crazy songs and monologues. He played several of the very top Blackpool venues, the last

GRAND THEATRE
P R O G R A M M E
MONDAY, AUGUST 13th and WEEK.   6-30 — TWICE NIGHTLY — 8-40.
PERSONAL VISIT OF
GRACIE FIELDS
AND STUPENDOUS SUPPORTING STAR VARIETY.

OVERTURE.
The Grand Theatre Orchestra.

1. MARTYN & FLORENCE,
   Comedy Jugglers.
2. MURRAY & COHAN,
   Sense and Nonsense.
3. THREE ADMIRALS,
   Commanders of Melody.
4. The Popular West-End Comedian,
   FREDDIE FORBES, supported by
   ANGELA BARRIE, presents 'A Quiet SPOT'

SELECTION.

5. THREE ABERDONIANS,
   Two Mean and a Girl.
6. JACK LE DAIR,
   The Amazing Trickologist.
7. BUCK WARREN & CHIC COOPER
   with PRIMROSE & PHIL in 'Let's Go.'
8. FREDDIE FORBES
   and ANGELA BARRIE again in 'Hearts.'
9. GRACIE FIELDS
10. THE ACT SUPERB
    Presented by TOM D. GRAY

INTERVAL.

Above: Gracie Fields was a huge favourite at the Grand Theatre from her first appearance in 1929.

Victoria Pier, Blackpool, (now the South Pier).

one being the Palace Theatre in 1926.

Another bill topper at the Palace Theatre later in 1935 was the brilliant harmonica player, Larry Adler, who had just arrived from America. He was a big hit in Blackpool and came back to the Palace, topping the bill, the following year and the year after. He moved to this country permanently in the late 1940s and was back again topping at the Palace in 1957. He later wrote and played the entire musical soundtrack for the film *Genevieve*.

A favourite music hall comedian, Billy Bennett played at the Palace in Blackpool for 22 years off and on, starting in the 1920s. His bill matter in the programmes suggested he was 'Almost a Gentleman'. His dress was a baggy oversize evening dress with brown boots, a woman's suspender as a watch fob, all topped off with a huge walrus moustache and his hair plastered down with an exaggerated quiff. He parodied famous songs and, particularly, Kipling poems, such as *Green Eye of the Little Yellow God* that became *The Green Tie of the Little Yellow Dog*. He delivered the nonsensical poems very rapidly and loudly. He was a big radio favourite in the 1930s and I know my father was a great fan and always laughed at Bennett's nonsense. He was also one half of a double act, Alexander and Mose, with another music hall favourite, Albert Whelan.

A great lady of the music halls was Florrie Forde, who was so fond of Blackpool that she managed to spend her birthday working at the Palace on no fewer than 22 occasions. In her young days she was a wonderful principal boy in her own pantomime productions, one of which included two artistes, Chesney Allen and Reuben Weintrop. She liked them both but suggested that Weintrop was not a good name for the music halls. 'What about Bud and my real surname, which is Flanagan?' she suggested. And that's how the great team of Flanagan and Allen was born. Florrie herself was Australian. She came

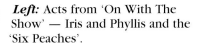

Left: Acts from 'On With The Show' — Iris and Phyllis and the 'Six Peaches'.

to England in 1897 and stayed for the remainder of her life. Her famous music hall songs included *Has Anyone Here Seen Kelly* and *Down at the Old Bull and Bush* and the reception was never so good as it was when she sang them in Blackpool.

Dave Morris was a comedian who not only played 13 consecutive seasons in Blackpool but was also a resident of the resort. He had suffered badly in the trenches in World War I and this encouraged him to work for many service charities during his career. His big break in Blackpool was in Lawrence Wright's 'On With The Show' and by 1938 was he topping variety bills. After starring in a season at the Opera House in the late 1940s he put on his own shows at the South Pier for five consecutive seasons. He had radio success with a series called *Club Night*, which was later transferred onto television. There followed another series called *The Artful Dodger*. Dave Morris was forever Blackpool.

What can one say about Frank Randle that hasn't been said before? He was a character made for the theatre and was just as mad off stage as he was on. He loved Blackpool audiences, who were prepared to ignore Randle's escapades, some of them with the forces of law and order — in fact he once said, 'Some of my best performances are in the Magistrates Court'. He was born illegitimately, in 1901 and between then and 1957, when he died of multiple causes, he made and lost various fortunes. Audiences would literally roll in the aisles at his antics. The police used to sit in the audience trying to find anything in his act that could put him in court. Nowadays it would not even warrant a mention.

One instance was when he had a fellow dressed in women's clothes on stage with him, holding a handbag. During the sketch Randle touched the fellow's arm and he was immediately reported for a homosexual activity and was up before the magistrates. He had his own show — *Randle's Scandals* — and he made over 20 films. He once smashed up a dressing room after an altercation with the

Cliff Shaw's 'Pleasure Crew', West End Pier, Morecambe, 1934.

management and once, to prove to the police he was not drunk, he performed a ballet dance along the Blackpool Promenade at five o'clock one morning.

Once, after he had smashed his car up, he said there had been a dangerous vehicle driving straight at him — it was a stationary tram. I met him once at an after-show party in Leeds, hosted by the mayor. The mayor said to Randle 'and what do you do?' Randle looked at the mayor for a minute and picked up a small trifle on a plate and pushed it into the mayor's face, with the words, 'That's what I do, and it don't half make them laugh.' He had a wonderful rubber face which several people have copied since, but never quite with the brilliance of Randle.

Another famous entertainer, the Tower organist, Reginald Dixon, was certainly 'Mr Blackpool' to millions of people for 40 years at the Tower Ballroom. *I Do Like to be Beside the Seaside*, became his signature tune not only for those millions who listened and danced to his playing on the Wurlitzer organ in the ballroom, but also to millions of radio listeners all over the world. Reginald Dixon was a gentleman, a great entertainer, and a long term resident of Blackpool. His grown-up families also have homes in the area.

Further up the northwest coast, **Morecambe** was the birthplace of one of our great English actresses, one who is just as much at ease with tragedy as she is with comedy — Dame Thora Hird has mastered both in her long career. Born just a few years before World War I, she made her debut at the age of three in one of her father's stage productions. Her many stage appearances in comedies with artistes such as Arthur Askey and Freddie Frinton in Blackpool, and in London's West End with the cream of British theatre, have endeared her to millions and have been a joy to watch. Dame Thora (but to her public still 'our Thora') has taken television in her stride too, particularly recently in Alan Bennett's *Talking Heads* series. She is as proud of Morecambe and its people as they are of her.

In the 1920s and 1930s, **Great Yarmouth** on the east Norfolk coast challenged Blackpool as a major seaside resort. It already had two fine piers, the Britannia and the Wellington, the Windmill Theatre on the Promenade, the Aquarium opposite the Britannia, and the Hippodrome Circus. Both piers were venues for pierrot troupes and concert parties, such as Reg Maddox's 'Evening Follies' at the Wellington Pier.

One of the comedians in 'Evening Follies' was Chris

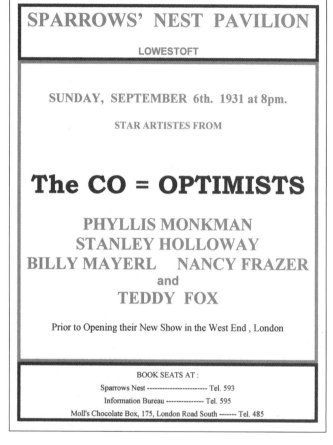

Above: Facsimile of a Davey Burnaby 'Co-Optimists' promotion from Lowestoft in 1931.

Wortman who had an unusual sideline. He was engaged to impersonate the voice of Al Jolson, the hugely popular American entertainer when the 'all talking, all singing' picture arrived in this country. Frank Maddox, Wortman's boss, had a cinema in the West Country that had not been wired for sound, so he engaged Wortman to sit in the pit with the orchestra and sing all Jolson's songs — something he did with commendable accuracy. Problems arose, however, when the projection equipment caused the film to vary its speed, and Chris and the band had to go slower or faster to synchronise with the film!

In 1930, a whisky firm erected a large electric cricket scoreboard next to the Wellington Pier for the whole of the test match series that summer, as England and Australia fought it out for the Ashes. There was huge

The Winter Gardens, Morecambe.

interest that year, particularly on 12 July at Headingley as the score of a young, first-time tourist to this country — the great Australian batsman Don Bradman — mounted towards the highest individual innings' total, then 325 runs. Bradman would eventually reach 334.

Later in the 1930s Walter Paskin's 'Come to the Show' came to the Wellington Pier Winter Gardens. This was a delightful building and Paskin's show complemented the venue with his beautifully dressed and artistically presented company. In Paskin's 1936 company was a very young dancer called Dora Bryan.

At **Gorleston**, Yarmouth's smaller neighbour, the Pavilion Theatre overlooked its lovely sandy beaches and presented some very good concert parties at that time. Early in the 20th century Carney and West's company was at the pavilion, and at the Olympia Quay Gardens (opposite the pavilion; it later became the Floral Hall and swimming pool) there was a company called the 'Ad-Lib Entertainers'. The pianist in that show was Jack Hylton whom I mentioned earlier.

In 1927, Elsie and Doris Waters took over the pavilion for the summer with their company, the 'Enthusiasts'. They made their presence felt on the halls and in particular on radio, with the two delightful characters 'Gert and Daisy'. Their brother, Jack Warner, didn't do too badly either. From very humble beginnings as a hotel entertainer at £4 a week, he rose to be a major cabaret artiste, film actor and, of course, *Dixon of Dock Green*.

In 1928, Frank Wilcock and Bob Rutherford came to the pavilion with their company. The pair became perhaps the most prolific writers of summer show material. Over the years I doubt if there was a concert party anywhere that did not use one of their sketches or concerted items — I've certainly performed more than one Wilcock and Rutherford sketch in my time.

Lowestoft was a large and busy fishing port so one would not have expected it to cater for holidaymakers in any great quantity; however, its record of entertainment is quite prolific. The South Pier Pavilion at Lowestoft was a concert party date in the 1920s, seeing many top acts including Richard Jackson's company. There was also a large open bandstand on the pier with the 'Commandores' Orchestra, conducted by Harry Davidson. Michael Mills relates that in July 1938 3,000 people crowded onto the pier to hear him.

The old pavilion fell into disrepair during the war years, but a new one was built in 1956; it was opened by the Duke of Edinburgh. All the big bands played at the pavilion, and the guests included Jimmy Young, Dennis Lotis, Lita Rosa, Craig Douglas and Brian Johnson. The list is like a 'Who's Who' of the music business.

Below: 'Come to the Show' at the Winter Gardens, Yarmouth.

The Floral Hall, Scarborough, 1937.

The Sparrow's Nest Gardens had been a concert party venue since just before the turn of the century and continued into the early 1900s. Just before World War I a grand concert pavilion was built on the site of the old tented pavilion. It was used to some extent during the war, but afterwards so many well known names played there that it is like turning the pages of an encyclopedia of entertainment of the 1920s and 1930s — with comedians of the day, singers, concert pianists, actors and well known artistes such as Paul Robeson, Dan Leno Jnr, Mark Harnburg, Clapham and Dwyer, Anton Dolin, Debroy Somers, Frank Forbes-Robertson, Vic Oliver, Elsie and Doris Waters and many others. When Elsie and Doris were playing their season there in 1939, the Royal Navy arrived during a performance and said they had come to take over the building and the surrounding gardens for the duration of the war. Consequently it became the headquarters of the RN Coastal Patrol Squadron and the Sparrow's Nest became HMS *Europa*.

One of the crew of *Europa* was Able Seaman Jon Pertwee; another was George Crow, and it was during this period at Lowestoft that they hurriedly put on some entertainment for their fellow shipmates. Jon, as he told me later, was doing the odd monologue and no doubt trying out some of his funny voices, and George Crow supplied the music. Several years later they met up again in Eric Barker's long running radio show *Waterlogged Spa* (Eric himself was an ex-Navy man) which was the spin-off from the wartime series *Mediterranean Merry-Go-Round*.

Waterlogged Spa was a fictional and not too efficient shore-based naval station in peacetime, with all sorts of illicit goings-on taking place, and a host of comical characters. They had probably drawn on their experiences at Lowestoft and elsewhere, and Jon, in particular, played some wonderfully eccentric people in that show. One, in particular, became very famous on radio — the Devonshire postman whose catch phrase was 'What does it matter what you do as long as you tear 'em up!' George Crow also joined *Waterlogged Spa* and created the 'Blue Mariners' Dance Orchestra.

Entertainment in **Scarborough** continued after World War I much as it had done before. The 'Fol-de-Rols' under the new management team of George Royle and Greatrex Newman was establishing itself and word got around to other resort managers who came to see the shows with a view to inviting them to produce elsewhere. Greatrex, or Rex as everybody called him, was not only

Above: No, not those Rolling Stones, although these were advertised as 'Always Ahead of the Times'. Richard Jerome's 'Rolling Stones' played Scarborough in 1937.

Right: The Futurist Buildings, Scarborough, incorporated the Futurist Cinema, and the Arcadia Theatre, buffet and restaurant. Owners — Catlin's Entertainments Ltd.

the keeper of the purse strings, but he also wrote a lot of the Fols' material, while George Royle got on with the overall production side. Rex was also writing for the famous 'Co-optimists', and they not only played seaside dates but also had 10 very successful seasons in London at the Winter Gardens Theatre, now the site of the new London Theatre. Another recipient of Rex's material was the 'Crazy Gang' led by Bud Flanagan and Chesney Allen who carried all before them at London's Palladium Theatre and the Victoria Palace.

Showtime Parade, Scarborough.

Apart from his touring pierrot companies, Will Catlin was looking to expand his interests in Scarborough. By the 1920s he had already built on the north shore his own Arcadia Theatre with a seating capacity of 3,000. This was only the beginning of his foreshore development. A restaurant was added to the Arcadia and then, in 1921, Catlin opened a huge cinema, the 'Futurist', again with a capacity of 3,000. He used his Arcadia not only for his own troupes but also for other touring shows.

Meanwhile, the 'Fol-de-Rols' still occupied the Floral Hall, although the emergence of the more sophisticated concert parties had started to push the previously established pierrots into the background in many resorts in the 1920s. Another important Scarborough venue, the Spa Theatre on the south shore has been used for seasonal shows and staged concerts along with the Spa Grand Hall and Spa Ballroom.

The New Grand Pavilion at **Bridlington** was built in the late 1930s to replace the old one destroyed by fire. For many years it housed summer shows of all descriptions. Now named Royal Hall, it and the Spa Theatre have been entertainment centres for all the big star names. Les Dawson, I know, loved the Spa and Ken Dodd has kept audiences up long after their bedtimes with his brilliance.

Ted Lune was another huge favourite for years — when he slipped his teeth out surreptitiously, the ladies in the audience screamed at his weird and wonderful facial expressions.

Fred Clements carried on producing shows at his Arcadia Theatre, **Skegness**, during the 1920s and 1930s right up until he sold it in 1935. He also produced a few shows in the Pier Pavilion, which was a flourishing summer date with popular companies, one of which was Ernest Binns' 'Arcadian Follies'. Much later the beautiful and elegant actress Kay Kendall (remember the film *Genevieve?*) used to watch her father Henry in revue there when she was a young girl. Stage and television actress Avril Angers was a summer revue dancer in one of the shows when she was quite young. Nowadays it is the Embassy Theatre complex that is the show date in Skegness, where nearly all the top names in entertainment have played giving audiences what they want, just as Fred Clements did all those years ago

The Lincolnshire coast was a good area for entertainment before and after World War I. Many of the artistes who played at Skegness moved farther up the coast to **Cleethorpes**, another popular area for concert parties such as Jimmy Slater's 'Super Follies'. Freddie Frinton, born in nearby Grimsby, was one of the artistes there before he went on to music hall and television fame. His most brilliant sketch, 'Dinner for One', is shown every New Year's Eve in Germany, with Freddie's slightly inebriated dialogue dubbed into German.

I played the pier at Cleethorpes and I remember the noise of the sea rushing in, making it a little difficult to hear what was being said on stage. Happy days!

Second World War

'The Day War Broke Out'

by Robb Wilton

At the outbreak of World War II, stage and film producer Basil Dean realised very quickly that there would be a need for some form of entertainment for the servicemen and women in the army garrisons, naval stations and RAF units around the country. Civilian morale was also very important and the factory workers turning out the planes, guns and shells needed for the war effort were to be included in the scheme. Dean took over the Theatre Royal, Drury Lane, in London as the headquarters for the Entertainments National Service Association the organisation that was to become better known as ENSA.

His first plan was to recruit some of the top names in the entertainment world, established performers such as George Formby, Gracie Fields, Flanagan and Allen, Vera Lynn and Tommy Trinder. He asked them if they were prepared to take part in his project and perform for the troops both at home and in France, where a large British Expeditionary Force was already dug in.

Dean needed both the co-operation of the artistes' agents and the War Office. An agreement was reached and before Christmas in 1939 some of the entertainers had already arrived in France. This continued all through the 'Phoney War' of early 1940, until the fall of Holland and France and the evacuation of Dunkirk forced ENSA artistes to leave mainland Europe. They would only return after D-Day in June 1944. Elsewhere, units from 'Stars in Battledress' and Ralph Reader's RAF 'Gang Shows', from the central pool of artistes, all servicemen and women, took their shows right up to the front line, often under fire. They carried on during the campaign in the Western Desert and in the jungles of Burma and the Far East, sometimes with hair-raising difficulties. Towards the end of the war, all the units came under one umbrella and were designated 'Combined Services Entertainment'.

None of this had been easy for artistes, going into unknown territory not knowing what they might find, but they were there to entertain and entertain they did! Sometimes they would play to an audience of a thousand or more in a garrison theatre or aircraft hangar. Another time it might just be a handful of men on a lonely gun-site 'somewhere in England'. A number of artistes also went to naval bases such as Scapa Flow off the north coast of Scotland where the Royal Navy's main striking force was stationed. The musical comedy star, Evelyn Laye, went there and she even paid her own expenses and those of the other artistes with her.

Towards the end of 1939 'Fol-de-Rols' producer Rex Newman was recruited by Basil Dean to help in what was growing into a very large organisation. Newman suggest-

The Inland Revenue Orchestra

President:
SIR CORNELIUS J. GREGG, K.B.E., C.B.

Vice-Presidents:
W. G. E. Burnett Esq.
S. P. Chambers, Esq., C.I.E.
Sir William E. Diggines.
C. E. Hidden, Esq.
P. Martin, Esq.
Sir Harry Nell.
F. N. D. Preston, Esq.
F. A. Slee, Esq., C.B.
C. H. Wakely, Esq.
A. S. Whitehead, Esq.

* * *

ORCHESTRAL CONCERT

PIER PAVILION, LLANDUDNO.
SUNDAY, DECEMBER 12th, 1943 at 7·30 p.m.
in aid of the
STALINGRAD HOSPITAL RELIEF FUND.

* * *

Solo Pianoforte .... ROY BROOKES
Conductor .... JOHN FRY

PROGRAMME, 3d.

Above: Shanklin theatre announcement, 1939.

Left: So that's what they did with our money!

The Bill Hall Trio in Italy in 1943 including a young
Spike Milligan on guitar. (How did he get in this book?)

Left: Brandon and Pounds'
'Out of the Blue' concert
party, Mersa Matruh,
1943, at the height of the
desert war.

ed it might be a good idea to send out to France a few established concert parties that had been playing summer seasons round our coasts for several years and were obviously very well organised. It was thought this might be a tricky undertaking and there was little enthusiasm for it at the War Office. It was difficult enough making sure a solo artiste was not put in any danger, but to look after a whole party of a dozen or more performers was another thing. However, Rex had his way and a party of 'Fol-de-Rols' was sent to France in 1939, although with a name change: 'Fol-de-Rols' was thought a little too whimsical, so the party was renamed the 'Scamps'.

They went out again in 1940 and one of their number, Peter Felgate, who had become an established member of the company, tells of an experience just before the fall of France. He was sitting in a café in Rouen when he heard on the wireless that all entertainers had now been evacuated and were on their way home to England. Peter did not wait to finish his cup of coffee but immediately started his long journey back to the French coast, having rounded up the rest of the company. They joined the long line of refugees making their way to any Channel port that might still be open. 'Most of the time,' he told me, 'was spent jumping in and out of ditches, dodging the machine-gun fire from the German planes overhead.' He finally managed to get back to England in time to answer his own call-up to the services.

One or two other concert parties did venture forth during the war — Ronnie Brandon and Dickie Pounds 'Out of the Blue' company which, among other places, travelled around the Western Desert. Reg Lever's 'Hello Happiness' was another, and so too the 'Balmorals'.

The war had been quite hairy for the entertainers in many ways, but all of them, star names and lesser known alike, stuck to their task, which at times, as several told me, was also real fun. There were one or two near tragedies — one in particular when a ship carrying entertainers and nurses to the Middle East was bombed and sunk in the Mediterranean. Luckily, they were all picked up by other ships in the area and continued on their way.

When the war finished, entertainment was organised for the British Occupation Forces in Europe. This was undertaken by Colonel Richard Stone, an actor before the war who had returned from active service with the Eighth Army in North Africa, and another actor, Ian Carmichael. They worked under the banner of Combined Services Entertainment, and even recruited actors and circus performers from Eastern European countries. Richard Stone became a well-known agent and producer once he was back in Civvy Street and Ian Carmichael became a popular stage and screen actor.

The subject of entertainment during World War II has been recorded in *Fighting for a Laugh* by Richard Fawkes and *Stars in Battledress* by Bill Pertwee.

The 'Co-Optimists' — Stanley Holloway is standing at far left; Davey Burnaby is standing third from left.

Top: Wilson James introduces his 'Gaities' in the 1920s.

Above: This happy little troupe is simply captioned as the 'Glamour' Concert Party on a postcard dated back into the 1920s.

1932's 'Arcadian Follies'.

Right: Ernest Binns, third from right in the front row, with his 'Arcadian Follies' in the 'Revelry of 1931'.

Left: 'We're free for the summer.' The 'Avonmores' in 1921.

Below: The 'West End Frolics' of 1930.

The audiences in the inter-war years were big and wanted to be entertained.

Right: A concert party song album cover featuring the master concert party writer Rex Newman.

Summer frocks and summer hats pick out a fashion-conscious 1930s' audience.

Above: Ronald Frankau's 'Blues'.

Left: Westbrook Pavilion (previously the Westonville Pavilion), Margate.

Betty Bruce, comedienne of the 'Ped'lers'.

Above: Leslie Fuller's 'Ped'lers' going strong in 1933 (programme for Clifton Concert Hall, Cliftonville).

Above Right: Ernest Binns presents the 'Arcadian Follies' at the Arcadian Pavilion, Morecambe, in 1935. Top of the solo stars — Albert Modley.

Right: Ernest Binns' Company.

Jack Sheppard's Entertainers for the 1920
Brighton season.

Above: 'Playtime Follies'
at St Leonards-on-Sea. Algy
More far left.

Above Left: Chirgwin's
concert party, with the
eponymous owner,
George Chirgwin, front
centre.

Left: Brighton's Palace
Pier.

Below: Brighton's
beautiful, ornate West
Pier.

Herbert Grove's 'Mag-Yars' concert party troupe. Far right, James Macleod.

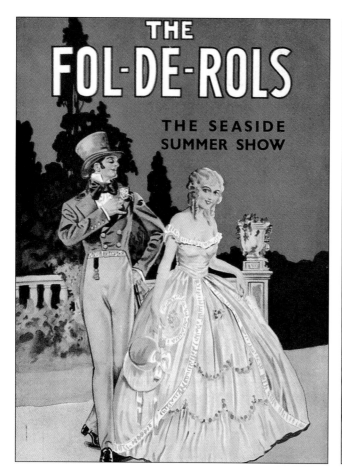

Above: Programme front for a mid-1930s 'Fol-de-Rols' seaside summer show at the Winter Garden, Eastbourne.

Above Right: Typical alfresco seaside entertainment — the multitudes watch 'Uncle Mac's Minstrels' at Broadstairs.

Right: Ventnor Pier. Sadly no more.

The 'Gay Cadets', Bournemouth 1925.

"TWINKLE."

FOUR CLARKSON ROSEBUDS
L.   Vera White, Marion Gordon,
    Rene Marsh, Sheila Downey.

SPECIALITY DANCES.
1 Stool Dance
2 Waltz Variation
3 Tambourine
4 Walking Stick Dance
5 Pyjamas
6 Spanish
7 Russian
8 Ballet
9 Buck Dance
10 Extra

:: BALLETS ::
1 Sports Ballet
        Rose & Mann
2 Toy Nursery
        George Buchanan
3 Rose Ballet
        Rose & Mann
4 Old Curiosity Shop
        Rose & Buchanan
5 Punch and Judy Show
6 Raindrops
7 Extra

Above: Programme for Shanklin Pleasure Pier's 1930 season. The attraction was Clarkson Rose's 'Twinkle' company.

Above Right: 'Twinkle' at Shanklin in 1930. These are the four 'Clarkson Rosebuds', Vera White, Marion Gordon, Rene Marsh and Sheila Downey.

Right: Arthur Askey (in glasses) was a great success in Shanklin. Also in this photo is Bernard Lee (third from left) who would play 'M' in the James Bond movies.

Willie Cave's pitch at high tide in Bournemouth.

Right: The early 19th century constructions at Bournemouth were a small wooden jetty later replaced by a longer one. In 1876 a storm rendered the latter unsafe for steamers and it was demolished. A new iron pier, designed by Eugenius Birch, opened in 1880, and shelters and a bandstand were added to the pier head. Further extensions and facilities were added in 1894 and 1905.

Corbyn Beach and Grand Hotel, Torquay.

Right: Plymouth — the pier promenade and the Hoe in the foreground.

Below Right: Torquay Pier and Harbour

Below Left and Right: A special broadcast from Brighton's Palace Pier in 1937 — note Tommy Trinder highlighted on page 19.

Weston-Super-Mare Pier.

Left: The 'Cabaret Kittens' featured at the Cosy Nook in Newquay. Centre, sitting, is Naunton Wayne.

Below Left: The 'Merryfolk' at Weston in 1928.

Below: Birnbeck Pier, Weston-super-Mare, 1896. Opened in 1867, Birnbeck Pier is famous for being the only seaside pier in Britain that actually went out to an island.

Below Right: 1933 programme front from the Floral Hall, Southport, where Sidney Ilott's 'Cabaret Follies' entertained the punters.

Roy Cowl's 'Queeries', Grove Park Pavilion, 1928.

Right: New Brighton's wooden pier was replaced by an iron structure in 1867. Varied attractions were offered from the start: a saloon, an observation tower, refreshment rooms and an orchestra, all later replaced. A pavilion was added, which became the base for the Adeler and Sutton pierrots from the early 1900s. The pier was closed in 1965, reopened in 1968, closed again in 1972 and demolished in 1977.

Above: An early 1900s view of Southport — pierrots give an alfresco show. The parasols are up, so it must be a sunny day. The sign above the stage identifies 3.30 and 7.30 shows.

Cliff Shaw and his 'Pleasure Crew', West End Pier,
Morecambe, 1934.

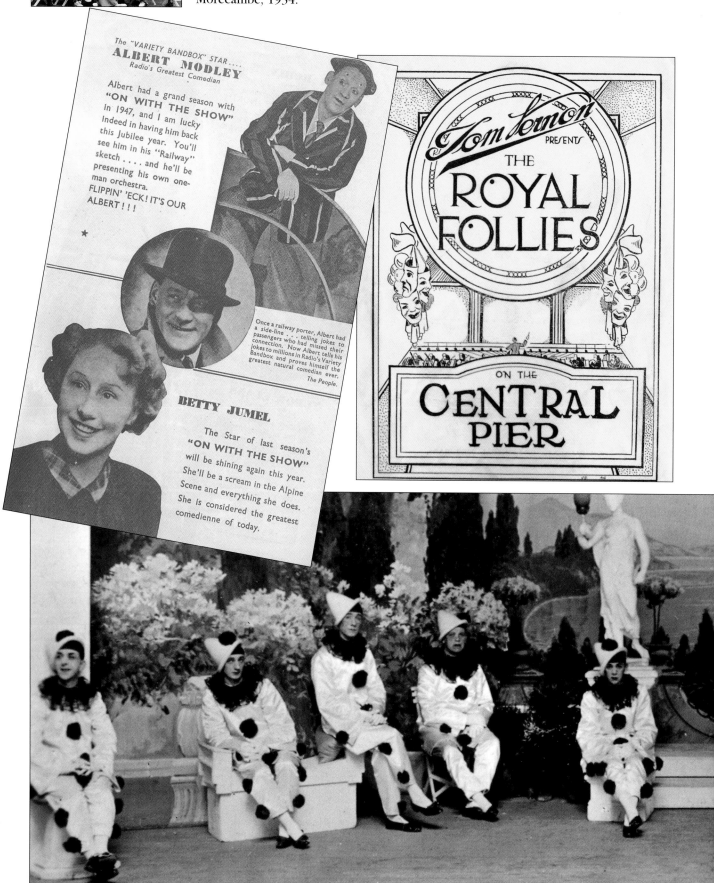

The "VARIETY BANDBOX" STAR....
ALBERT MODLEY
Radio's Greatest Comedian

Albert had a grand season with
"ON WITH THE SHOW"
in 1947, and I am lucky
indeed in having him back
this Jubilee year. You'll
see him in his "Railway"
sketch . . . . and he'll be
presenting his own one-
man orchestra.
FLIPPIN' 'ECK! IT'S OUR
ALBERT ! ! !

*

Once a railway porter, Albert had
a side-line . . . telling jokes to
passengers who had missed their
connection. Now Albert tells his
jokes to millions in Radio's Variety
Bandbox and proves himself the
greatest natural comedian ever.
The People.

BETTY JUMEL

The Star of last season's
"ON WITH THE SHOW"
will be shining again this year.
She'll be a scream in the Alpine
Scene and everything she does.
She is considered the greatest
comedienne of today.

Tom Vernon PRESENTS
THE
ROYAL
FOLLIES

ON THE

CENTRAL
PIER

The 'Fol-De-Rols', Floral Hall, Westcliff-on-Sea.

Left: Mrs Leo Bliss's 'Busy Bees', Whitley Bay, 1925.

Opposite page, Above Left: Albert Modley and Betty Jumel in a postwar Blackpool production.

Opposite page, Above Right: The 1932 season on Blackpool's Central Pier boasted the 'Royal Follies' and included in the cast Sam Rayne who came 'from the Emerald Isle and is a broth of a bhoy, intoirely!'

Below: Catlin's 'Royal Pierrots' at Scarborough in the early part of the 20th century.

The 'Pierrot Players' of 1929.

Right: 1920s' view of Hunstanton Pier from Pier Green.

Below: Clay Thomas and Stewart Goss's 'Seamews' played Hunstanton in 1931.

Bottom: Promenade and sands at Redcar in the 1930s. In the distance Redcar Pier; in the foreground the 'Optimists' on the beach.

Happy Valley, Westcliff-on-sea.

Above: Elsie and Doris Waters' 'Enthusiasts' at Gorleston-on-sea, 1927.

Top: Rex 'Tubby' Harold at far right in this 1930s' Gorleston view.

Above Left: A souvenir programme from Gorleston Pavilion.

Left: Gorleston beach and bandstand.

'Happy Days are here again'

The spectacular comes to the seaside

After the war, holidaymakers started flocking to the coastal resorts, small and large, not just because it had been a long time since they had seen a promenade without barbed wire on it, but also because the demobbed servicemen were back together with their families. What better place to feel again part of the family than in the happy-go-lucky atmosphere of a seaside resort, where they could relive the pleasures they had experienced before 1939. Children born just before the war or during the conflict hadn't any experience of the seaside, so the end of the 1940s was an exciting journey of discovery for them.

Pamela Cundell

Even a walk by the sea or a stroll along the pier — those few that had opened up again — was exciting. The smell of ozone and of the cockle and whelk stalls made you feel good; a paddle in the water, with dad in his braces and trousers turned up to the knees and mum with her dress tucked up into her knickers, was a sight repeated all around British coastal beaches. Noisy children armed with buckets and spades were everywhere, making sandcastles and covering dad in sand up to his waist, while mum arranged the picnic they'd brought with them, busily trying to keep the sand out of the sand-wiches. There were the donkey rides, Punch and Judy shows, and the eagerly anticipated ice cream vendors that hadn't been seen for several years of course. It was a time of general liberation as people looked forward to the sec-ond half of the century with hope and anticipation.

I witnessed a lot of this at first hand as I was living at Westcliff-on-Sea in Essex at the time, and I can remember seeing the day trippers getting on the trains in their hundreds for the journey back to London. If it had been a really hot day their faces would be beetroot red, even those of the children and babies who would be crying amidst all the hustle and bustle at the station. If you were staying for, say, a week, a stroll in the late evening along the cliff walk illuminated gently with coloured lights hanging in the trees, gave a touch of romance.

There was the Kursaal, a huge funfair complex at Southend that had every conceivable amusement for the holidaymaker to enjoy, and at night there was the Kursaal

ballroom with all the big bands of the day. This was a favourite venue for some of us lads — after we had played cricket on a Saturday — to meet the girls who lived in the area.

The pier had opened up again with many attractions, including the concert party at the end of it. A famous one there was Wilby Lunn's 'Bubbles'. Lunn was in partnership with Will Seymour, who was also his principle comedian. Pamela Cundell, who was in the company at one time, said:

'The theatre was above the line carrying the pier train from the shore end and if you were telling a gag you had to wait for the train to go through before you delivered the tag line of it as the noise of the train made it impos-sible for the audience to hear anything. If the train was going slower than usual you couldn't even start the gag at all until it had rumbled on its way.'

Southend Pier was also a docking point for the steamers bringing day trippers from London's Tower Bridge, as was Margate on the opposite coast in Thanet. Another busy pier for the London Steamer Service was Clacton-on-Sea. In fact all the piers around our coasts then had a good steamer trade, even if some of their journeys were only short.

Come the beginning of the 1950s and changes were already happening. Even the holidaymakers were chang-ing their styles of dress, particularly at the seaside. The young ladies were taking to wearing two-piece swimming costumes, not quite bikinis but not far off; and as they walked along the promenade, they brought gasps from some of the older generation, with mum tut-tutting and father trying to look away before he got an admonishing glare from his wife. It was also the start of the teddy boy era, with the lads sporting themselves at the resorts in their long coats, tight trousers and shoelace thin ties.

It was also the time of change for seaside entertain-ment. Subtle differences had been creeping in for a few years at Blackpool, and in Lawrence Wright's 'On With

Butlin's Ocean Hotel, Brighton.

the Show' at the North Pier, they had started to bring in the star names famous from radio, records and some television programmes. This trend was to continue and develop with the beginning of commercial television in 1955. Another show producer who had always looked forward was Will Catlin, he of the Scarborough Pierrot companies. He now started putting on new type productions under the title of 'Catlin's Show Time'.

It was, however, two particular men who were to make the changes in seaside entertainment even more acute — Billy (later Sir) Butlin and Bernard (later Lord) Delfont.

Butlin's

Billy Butlin changed the habits of millions of postwar British holidaymakers in a most dramatic and ambitious style. He arrived from Canada in the mid-1930s as a young man and, with only a few pounds in his pocket, set up two or three fairground stalls, not far from Fred Clements Arcadia Theatre in Skegness. Butlin would draw the attention of Clements' audiences as they spilled out of the theatre by him ringing a bell and inviting them to try their luck on his hoop-la stall and such like. He was a sharp observer of holidaymakers' habits, and he noticed that on wet days (of which our seaside seems to get more than its fair share at times), families with children were wandering about in raincoats with nothing to do and were not allowed to go back to their bed and breakfast and 'high tea' guest houses until 5pm. The landladies didn't want them cluttering up their premises, getting in the way of the cooking and cleaning.

Billy Butlin thought that, if the holidaymakers had all they needed under one roof, their problems would be solved. If one camp could provide chalet-style sleeping accommodation — the type he'd seen in Canada — plus restaurants, bars, shops, childrens' play areas and entertainment, the holidaymakers would be happy.

In 1936 he bought some land in Skegness and proceeded to see if his gamble would pay off by putting his ideas into practice. Pay off it did, right from the start with his first camp which opened in 1937. The establishment was commandeered during the war by the armed services and was returned to him together with a compensation fee from the government. Billy used the money to buy more land and build more camps — Filey on the Yorkshire coast, Ayr in Scotland, Clacton, Bognor Regis, Minehead, Pwllheli, Barry Island. All these plus some large hotels he had taken over at Cliftonville and

Brighton. The backbone of his staff at the camps were the famous Redcoats. My word did they work hard, six days a week from 8am until midnight. They were responsible for keeping the campers happy — telling them at breakfast what events would be taking place during the day. There was always a range: the knobbly knees competition, that for the most beautiful grandmother, the childrens' talent contest, the swimming pool races for all ages and, on top of that, rehearsing and performing in the Butlin Revues, once, twice and sometimes three times nightly. Then going into the late night bars to make sure the campers had enjoyed their day. If there were any dissatisfied customers they tried to sort out their problems for them.

Roy Hudd, who was a young Redcoat said, 'At the end of the day you were absolutely knackered'. Other Redcoats who got onto the very first rung of the entertainment ladder through Butlin's were David O'Marney (later comedian Dave Allen), Harry Webb (Cliff Richard's real name), Des O'Connor and Charlie Drake, and — 'Didn't they do well', as Bruce Forsyth would later say. My son, actor James Pertwee, was a Redcoat when he was 17 and he said, 'The regime was pretty tough.'

I had a long contract with Butlin's as part of their celebrity line up to do Sunday concerts and weekends at Easter and Christmas. Sometimes we would do four shows a night when the camps had 8,000 occupants, 2,000 a performance in their large and well-equipped theatres, complete with a full orchestra.

There was a printed notice to all performers on the side of the stage which read, 'We will not tolerate bad language or blue gags at any price.' I don't think this applied so much later on when the big celebrity acts came in to do 30 or 45-minute spots in the ballrooms late at night. When you were performing in the theatres (and Roy Hudd confirms this), you would suddenly get a loudspeaker announcement in the audience, saying, 'There's a baby crying in chalet 21,' and up would jump mum or dad and off they'd go, climbing over people to sort out little Johnny in their chalet. Everything was very well organised at Butlin's.

Other types of camp sprang up after the war: Pontin's, Warner's, and several others, but Billy Butlin had really led the way. The television series *Hi-de-Hi* was a very accurate portrayal of holiday camp life. It was written by Jimmy Perry, who had been a Butlin Redcoat, and David Croft, who produced some of the camp shows presented by Richard Stone.

A Bernard Delfont production.

Lord Delfont

As well as Billy Butlin, Bernard Delfont realised that the British public, having experienced the resurgence of seaside holidays after the war, would want more than concert party entertainment once the novelty of visiting the seaside in the late 1940s had worn off. The concert parties had reigned supreme in the 1920s and 1930s but Delfont had thought carefully about the future of broadcasting and the imminent advent of commercial television (it eventually came about in 1955). Furthermore people were beginning to spend their money on a few home luxuries and even owning a car. Holiday brochures were also starting to drop through our letterboxes, telling us that Spain, France and places further afield were ready and waiting for us to spend our holidays with them. So the seaside shows had to sharpen up to the competition and give the public big names in their programmes to keep the resorts full in the summer months.

Delfont was already an established agent, with his colleague Billy Marsh, and his brothers, Lew and Leslie Grade. They had a large business with several important performers on their books, but Bernard Delfont was already a respected West End show producer, so he had a reputation for being able to bring his expertise to the larger resorts such as Blackpool, Bournemouth, Torquay, Scarborough and Yarmouth, and to a lesser extent Weymouth and Bridlington. He wanted to bring some of the well known radio performers and later the television personalities to the seaside.

Practically every major star would sooner or later appear in a Delfont production at one time or another. The shows were well produced with plenty of glamour and two or three top names in each show to bring in the customers. Blackpool, with its piers, the Opera House, Grand Theatre and other venues often all ran Delfont shows. Bernard later became Chairman of First Leisure Corporation, who took complete control of Blackpool's piers and the Tower complex and also the piers at

Eastbourne, Llandudno and Southsea. Money was then available for some refurbishment of these venues.

Delfont had an extraordinary life, after coming to England as a very young refugee from Russia and performing a variety act on the halls, to the great showman in the business of entertainment that he loved. We will come back to this amazing man later.

We start our circuit around Britain on the south coast in this chapter and where better to begin than in **Bournemouth**, which has been blessed with excellent climate, golden sands, beautiful cliff walks and excellent hotels. But has it got complacent? Far from it — Bournemouth has kept abreast of the times with a varied selection of restaurants, excellent shopping facilities, theme and leisure parks — not forgetting the nearby Poole Arts Centre, it seems Bournemouth would appear to have everything. Its abundance of entertainment — provided by star names attracted to the Pavilion, the Winter Gardens, the Pier Theatre and now the marvellous new International Centre — is really the icing on the cake.

Those star names love playing Bournemouth theatres. Actress Su Pollard told me, 'There's always something to look forward to when you know you are going to be working there. The club nightlife where the pros can gather after the show, they always make you welcome and they become your friends.'

I asked her then if it was her favourite resort. She hesitated a little — because

Su Pollard.

HAROLD FIELDING in association with GEORGE and ALFRED BLACK presents

THE BIG SHOW OF 1960

1. **OVERTURE** The Big Show Orchestra under the direction of Danny Walters

2. **"THE OPENING OF THE SHOW"**
   (Designed by Alec Shanks)
   (Costumes by Erte)
   (Music and Lyrics by Cyril Ornadel and David Croft)
   THE BILL SHEPHERD SINGERS
   THE JOHN TILLER GIRLS
   PRUDENCE POTTER
   and
   DORA BRYAN
   introducing
   AL READ

3. THE THREE GHEZZIS

4. **"JOLLIJAUNTS"** (by Arthur Macrae)
   Mavis Davies ... ... **DORA BRYAN**
   Alice ... ... PRUDENCE POTTER

5. **"WONDERLAND OF THE DEEP"** (Designed by Erte)
   (Music and Lyrics by Phil Park)
   (a) THE BLUE LAGOON
   The Sponge Diver ... ... DAVID ROWLEY
   The Boy ... ... CHRISTOPHER WALKER
   (b) TWENTY FATHOMS DOWN (An Under Water Fantasy)

6. **"THE LATE-COMERS"**
   Police Constable ... ... JOHN LUCAS
   Police Inspector ... ... FRED STONE
   One of the Lads ... ... **AL READ**
   His Pal ... ... RICHARD LANCASTER
   The Young Lady ... ... PRUDENCE POTTER

7. DORA BRYAN

8. **"THE SENSATIONAL WALTZING WATERS"**
   (Devised by Jimmy Currie)

———
INTERVAL
———

9. **"TOTEM RITUAL"** (Costumes designed by Alec Shanks)
   (Music and Lyrics by Cyril Ornadel and David Croft)
   THE BILL SHEPHERD SINGERS
   THE JOHN TILLER GIRLS

10. **"THE TROUBLE WITH MISS MANDERSON"**
    (by Alan Melville)
    Miss Smart ... ... PRUDENCE POTTER
    Dr. Webster ... ... FRED STONE
    Miss Manderson ... ... **DORA BRYAN**

11. MARTY WILDE and the Wildcats

12. **"A ROSE BOUQUET"** (Designed by Alec Shanks)
    THE JOHN TILLER GIRLS
    (Dance routine arranged by Barbara Aitken)

Left: Harold Fielding's production for the 1960 season at the Opera House, Blackpool.

Below: Sing-along-a-Max.

she still has a soft spot for Mablethorpe, but then agreed. Near Skegness, Mablethorpe was where she won a talent contest at the Sand Castle Venue near the beach when she was quite young, singing *I Want to Be Bobby's Girl*. She said, 'That's what gave me the ambition to become a professional,' and after a season or two with the co-operative amateur theatricals in Nottingham, that is what she did, and aren't we all glad. Su has given us all so much pleasure with her TV appearances and some wonderful stage performances. I have spent quite a number of years working with her since we first met in pantomime at the Pavilion in Bournemouth.

Quite a few artistes have made their home in Bournemouth. One who enjoys everything about it is Max Bygraves. He said:

'My favourite resort has to be Bournemouth. I've been coming to the place since my early days of touring. The digs we used were always a bit more expensive than elsewhere, but were very clean, the food was tasty, the sea air wonderful, and the shows were only once nightly too.

'When I did a season there the whole family would

Detail from a programme for Sandown Pavilion,
Isle of Wight.

come down and spend the summer, the children always said it was special to them.

'In 1969 when I was appearing at the Winter Gardens I spied a house I liked and we have lived here for the past 30 years. Today I love it even more.'

If I were to comment on Bygraves the performer, I would probably only repeat what has already been said about him. I first saw Max on the Judy Garland bill at the London Palladium (this was the occasion when Judy tripped on her entrance and landed on her bottom). The moment Max appeared he communicated with his audience, and his easy going style made you just sit back and enjoy everything he did.

I should like to quote from a Bournemouth programme which shows the extent of his work:

'There are no entertainers with his pedigree today. 19 Royal Variety shows, 31 gold discs for his sing-along recordings, voted twice as Personality of the Year by the Variety Club. His shows at the London Palladium and Victoria Palace are too numerous to mention. Films, television, Broadway with Judy Garland and now travelling the world — Australia, New Zealand, Hong Kong Canada, etc. There is nothing this fellow doesn't know about show business.'

I wonder if many people are aware that Tony Hancock was 'theatrically' born in Bournemouth when his parents were running a hotel there. They were friendly with a good old pro called George Fairweather and asked him to give Hancock some advice about going into show business. Tony was at that time doing one or two small gigs around the town and he always said that the advice George Fairweather gave him stood him in good stead in his future work as a professional.

The number of actors that have enjoyed playing at the Pier Theatre over the years is considerable. Dear old Sid James, Barbara Windsor, Terry Scott, June Whitfield, Jeffrey Holland and the TV casts of *Hi-de-Hi*, *It Ain't 'Arf 'Ot Mum* and *Allo, Allo*, have all played there.

This year (1999) one of the great farces of all time will be at the Pier Theatre, Ray Cooney's *Run for Your Wife*, which has a special place in my heart because, throwing modesty to the wind, I created the part of Sergeant Porterhouse in the original London production in 1983. I've played it many times since, in London as well as a season in Canada. It has been successful all over the world since it was first produced and I'm sure it will be a winner in Bournemouth too.

The Simmons Brothers, Alan and Keith, recent stars of several of the Cromer shows, knocked off the rough edges of their early entertainment endeavours on the **Isle of Wight** in the 1960s, playing in holiday camps. At that time they were featuring their singing more than their comedy and, in fact, had made a record for the Pye label produced by Tony Hatch. (He of the *Neighbours* signature tune and *Downtown*.) However, comedy was calling them

Above Right: The esplanade and pier looking towards Culver cliffs, Sandown.

Right: Shanklin Pier on the Isle of Wight, also alas, sadly no more.

The Simmons brothers, Keith and Alan.

and in 1973 they did a season at the Shanklin Pier with their comedy routines firmly in place. Then in 1984 they appeared at the Sandown Pavilion alongside the wonderful impressionist, Janet Brown (who could forget her Mrs. Thatcher?) and Bernie Clifton — plus ostrich. This time Bernie had with him a full sized plastic pig's head and put it in the girls' toilet bowl. Keith said, 'you could have heard the screams on the mainland!' I wonder whether Bernie shouldn't work with a pig instead of an ostrich!

The island certainly has some lovely memories for my wife and me. We did a season at the Sandown Pavilion in 1964, and the show was called *Merry-Go-Round*. Don Moody was the entertainments manager at that time, and what a wonderful character he was. He was known throughout the UK and would visit all the resorts looking for likely artistes who would fit into the shows on the island. The artistes who played there subsequently became his friends and we all became known as the 'Moody Minstrels'.

It was a very hot summer in 1964 and consequently the business could have been better, but it didn't seem to worry Don too much. We used to go out after the show to the local hotels where the various coach parties were staying. The visitors liked to meet the entertainers and Don said it was good public relations. They had plays on during the week at the Shanklin Theatre (it was formerly the Town Hall), but on Sunday nights the big stars would appear at Shanklin and Sandown.

The artistes in the first half at Sandown would leap into a taxi in the interval and make for Shanklin, where they would perform in the second half. Meanwhile, the first half at Shanklin would make for Sandown to do the second half there, passing the others' taxi *en route*. If all this sounds confusing, well sometimes it did get a little

A 'Masquerade' programme.

Above: The Esplanade Theatre, Bognor Regis, at night. If you look closely, the author's name is on the canopy.

Right: The summer season at the Esplanade Theatre in 1968 was the 'Bouquets'.

ESPLANADE THEATRE BOGNOR REGIS
Entertainments Manager: C. J. POWELL F.I.M.E.
June 15th, 1968 For Summer Season
THE GLAMOROUS SUMMER SHOW
The Bouquets
PROGRAMME 6ᴰ

hectic, especially if an act had a lot of props. But usually it worked very well.

My cousin Jon Pertwee came to do one of the Sundays and stayed at our flat. We had our dog Bilko with us and he rather took a fancy to Jon and wouldn't get off his bed. I went in the next morning to find Bilko stretched out on the bed and Jon asleep in his basket. Fortunately it was a large dog basket!

Dick Emery was a regular Sunday visitor and we spent a few jolly nights at his hotel after the show. In fact, we made many friends on the island during our stay in 1964, and we still keep in touch in particular with one family, the Snellings, Tony and Sybil. Sybil gave birth to a girl that summer, so of course it was a good excuse for celebrating! That little girl, Deborah, is now a mum herself with two delightful children. How time flies!

Jimmy Tarbuck has a great affection for the island. His visit in 1964 was the first time he had topped a bill since compèring the show *Sunday Night at the London Palladium*. He was immensely popular and the audience were keen to see him 'in the flesh'. My wife, who was also appearing in the Sunday show, had the honour of introducing him and she remembers his reception was deafening. She and Jimmy also shared the taxi to Shanklin after the interval

— another happy memory. Hasn't Jim done well since then, not just as a top performer, but as a great golfer on the celebrity circuit. He's a nice, cheery bloke to know, is Jim.

Finally, I must mention someone who became a great buddy during our season in 1964, Frankie Holmes. He used to refer to himself as 'Frantic Francis' and had a mischievous sense of fun. He was really a comedy magician, but would literally turn his hand to anything and we had many laughs together that year. I saw him not long ago, at Cromer with, would you believe, the Simmons Brothers, and after all this time he was still as funny and frantic as ever!

Jersey has always been an attractive and delightful place for a holiday, with its rugged coastline and glorious beaches, the continental atmosphere and nightlife. The Opera House (at present closed for a major refurbishment programme) was a venue for plays and pantomimes; Swansons and Sunshine Hotels provided lavish cabaret-style entertainment, and the Watersplash concentrated on music and band shows.

Tony Hancock.

Many of our star names have played the venues there. I would just like to mention the very good amateur group the 'Island Players' whom I have had the pleasure of seeing on more than one occasion.

Jersey as an island became more widely known through the very popular BBC TV series *Bergerac*, starring John Nettles and Terence Alexander. It has had many famous residents in the past — Sir Bill and Lady Butlin made their home on Jersey for many years.

Brighton in the 1960s was a really swinging place. My wife and I were living there at the time, just as clubs for all tastes and ages sprang up. Both the piers, the Palace and the West Pier, provided entertainment; the famous Brighton Hippodrome was still staging some great shows and the Theatre Royal had all the pre-West End plays to see. The 1960s were certainly exciting with extreme highs and lows. I particularly remember the Profumo affair, the Great Train Robbery, the assassination of President Kennedy, the mini skirt and long boots, the coming of the four lads from Liverpool — and that irreverent television show, *That Was the Week That Was*.

My wife, Marion, did a season at the West Pier Concert Hall in 1965, and I joined the show the following year. It was a great season: the houses were always full, the atmosphere was great, and the audience sat at tables being able to enjoy a glass of wine or whatever while the show went on. The guv'nor was Alan Gale, and he had a long experience of summer shows.

One of my happy memories of that summer was the night in July that our son was born. I remember it so well.

I had phoned the hospital during the evening to find out how things were going but there was still no news. Then, just before the interval, Alan Gale rushed onto the stage in the middle of one of my routines and stopped the show. He said, 'Ladies and gentlemen, excuse the interruption, but I have to tell you that Bill's wife has just presented him with a bouncing baby boy.' Well you should have heard the audience; drinks started coming up, of which I drank one or two, the rest I was passing on to the others in the cast and then to the band. A jolly night was had by all I can tell you!

Alan Gale was a real character. He used to go out during the interval and tell the audience that the show would only recommence when all the ice creams had been sold! He was obviously on commission. He was very paternal towards his artistes, however, and they all loved him. He revelled in the fact that he was always called the 'Master'.

There were a lot of other theatre folk living in Brighton at that time — Laurence Olivier, Flora Robson, Kenneth Horne, Dora Bryan, Alan Melville, Hermione Baddley, Terence Rattigan, and many more writers and journalists, one of them that nice chap Jack Tinker. Many of them used to bring their friends in to see the show when they were down for the weekend, and they all enjoyed the relaxed, happy-go-lucky atmosphere.

Below: The West Pier, Brighton in the 1960s. The Palace Pier is in the background.

Dad's Army at the seaside as a stage show musical at the Theatre Royal, Brighton, 1976.

Left: A Butlin redcoat group at Pwllheli in the 1950s. Standing, third from the right, is Jimmy Perry, who along with David Croft wrote such fantastic TV successes as *Dad's Army* and *Hi-de-Hi*.

Below: The Maple Leaf Four.

Dick Emery did a season at the Palace Pier Theatre in a full scale production and later on Tommy Trinder was there with a great singing group, the Maple Leaf Four. The Maples started out when four young ex-servicemen met up in a show just after World War II, and found that their voices blended well in close harmony. They decided to join forces and form an act — the Maple Leaf Four was the result, and not only did they appear in all the major theatres in variety and revue, they were also popular on radio, with their own show, the long running *Smoky Mountain Jamboree*. They made many recordings and television appearances, and were in great demand as a cabaret act.

They made their stage debut in Brighton in a revue called *The Town Roars* at the Hippodrome in June 1947. Starring in the show were Nat Mills and Bobbie, hugely popular on radio during the war, and even funnier on stage. The show was presented by the legendary George Black's two sons, George and Alfred Black. George Black junior was a captain in the army 'Stars in Battledress' unit and had first spotted the Maple Leaf boys' potential when they were under his command.

The following year saw the group in Blackpool for the summer at the Grand Theatre for Henry Hall. In the cast were Ted Ray, Jill Manners and a young Wilfred Brambell (later to find fame as old man Steptoe) the show, *Something in the Air*, was produced by Dick Hurran. Two years later, the boys were back in Brighton, again at the Hippodrome, this time with Norman Evans in *Over the Garden Wall*.

Two of the Maple Leaf Four, John and Norman MacLeod, liked Brighton so much that they decided to make their home in the area and brought up their fami-

Brighton Hippodrome programme from 1950.

lies there. Later in the group's career, they appeared many times at the Dome, and in the late 1960s did that season on the Palace Pier with comedian Tommy Trinder. This show was transferred to the Hippodrome, Eastbourne, the following year, where it broke all records.

When the boys finally decided to call it a day, the baritone, Norman MacLeod, went into the musical *Mame*, starring Ginger Rogers, at Drury Lane. Brother John, meanwhile, branched out as a song writer. He had always arranged all the music for the act, but now was penning such hits as *Let the Heartaches Begin* and *Baby Now That I've Found You*. Perhaps the Brighton air had something to do with their success!

If anyone thinks that **Worthing** is still in the era when it was known as a retirement resort, they would have to think again visiting the town today. It has moved on with the times as every other seaside town has, but has managed to keep a few of the good things of the past as well.

The Pier Pavilion Theatre still to this day has its great musical concerts. Into the 1960s and 1970s it still had visits from the old faithful summer revues such as 'Twinkle' and the 'Fol-de-Rols'. My late cousin, Jon Pertwee, was in a Richard Stone production there in the late 1960s. It still stages big variety shows as it has done in the past. I've played there in one of them, a happy week with Norman Vaughan and Billy Burden (what a character he was!). The Connaught Theatre has its fair mix of traditional plays and new works. Both the Pavilion and the Assembly Rooms have staged the orchestras of Ray Mcvay and Joe Loss, the modern music of the Marmalade, and special theme evenings such as the 1950s with Marty Wilde and the Wild Cats. My niece now lives in Worthing and I can recommend some good eateries and pubs to enjoy.

This is all a far cry from when I used to come into Worthing on the No 1 bus from Storrington at the beginning of the war. There was barbed wire all along the promenade, but if you were lucky you could still buy a home-made ice cream from a small cafe next to Southdown Bus Depot on the front. I do remember being bought some clothes at Kinch and Lack, and Mr Barnes' radio shop opposite the Town Hall where he demonstrated a newfangled machine called television. It had moving pictures you could see. Little did I know then that I would one day be one of those moving images on the screen. Where was the fortune teller?!

I do have a sneaking feeling of nostalgia when I drive down the dual carriageway from Washington into Worthing. I'm going to do it by bus again one of these days, if they're still running. Incidentally, my brother's name is on the war memorial in the town — Pilot Officer J. R. Pertwee, killed 1941. We were living just down the road in Findon at the time.

In 1948 someone arrived in **Eastbourne** who was eventually to be given the title 'Mr. Eastbourne'. His name was Sandy Powell, an already established comedian through the huge number of radio broadcasts, records (one of them in the 1930s sold a million!), and a lot of stage experiences, both in summer shows and variety. Sandy joined Walter Fellows's summer show at the Pier Theatre in 1948 and this was the start of his popularity in the resort over the next 20 years or

Norman Meadow.

GREATREX NEWMAN and HUGH CHARLES
present

The Fol-de-Rols

The Famous Song and Laugh Show
With New Fun! . . . New Faces! . . . New Airs! . . . New Graces!
Sketches and Lyrics by GREATREX NEWMAN and PHILIP WHITLEY
Mon.-Fri. at 7.45; Sat. 5.30 and 8.10. Matinee: Wed. at 2.30

This is
**PROGRAMME
No. 2**

**PROGRAMME
No. 3**
commences
Thursday next

PART I

1. "THE FOL-DE-ROLS" says "HOW D'YOU DO"

2. And take a "HOLIDAY CRUISE"

3. "HEADIN' FOR LOUISVILLE"
Lucy Fenwick, Brian Hill and the girls.

4. DON SMOOTHEY

5. "INSTANT TEA"
Waitress .... Kathleen West
Man .... John Lesley
Woman .... Maggie MacDonald

6. "A WINDMILL IN AMSTERDAM"
Lucy Fenwick and Nina Brown, Suzanne Beaumont, Wanda Bailey, Linzi Winsper, Denise Lucking, Rosemarie Sellwood

7. "SPRING IS IN THE AIR"

8. SANDY POWELL

9. "A DEGAS PICTURE"
Madame .... Kathleen West
Pupil .... Lucy Fenwick

10. DON SMOOTHEY assisted by John Lesley

11. "NOT SO MERRIE ENGLAND"

INTERVAL

PART II

12. TWO GRAND PIANOS plus JIMMY BAILEY and JENNIFER PARTRIDGE

13. "HIRE-PURCHASE STORES"
Couple .... Don Smoothey, Maggie MacDonald
Salesman .... John Lesley

14. KATHLEEN WEST

15. "WEDGWOOD"

16. MAGGIE MACDONALD

17. "TEA TABLE TATTLE"
Host .... Don Smoothey
Guests .... Sandy Powell, John Lesley

18. "DREAMS"
Singers—Clifton Todd, Roger de Courcey, Maggie MacDonald
Dancers—Susan Markwell, Lucy Fenwick, Brian Hill and Nina Brown, Suzanne Beaumont, Wanda Bailey, Linzi Winsper, Denise Lucking, Rosemarie Sellwood

19. "LOVE'S LABOUR LOST"
Him .... John Lesley
Her .... Kathleen West

20. SANDY POWELL

21. "THE STARS STILL SHINE"

NATIONAL ANTHEM

At the Pianos ...... JIMMY BAILEY and JENNIFER PARTRIDGE

At the Drums ...... PETER COLBURT

Music by HARRY TAIT and PHILLIP CHARLES
Dances arranged by CHERRY WILLOUGHBY
PRODUCTION BY PETER FELGATE
Puppets by Bob Pelham

The Management reserve the right to alter or omit any item.

FOR HUGH CHARLES AND THE FOL-DE-ROLS LTD.
Production Supervisor .... Peter Felgate | Stage Manager .... Howard Eastman
Assistant to Production Supervisor | Deputy Stage Manager ...... Michael Pannell
.... Howard Eastman | Wardrobe Mistress .... Gillian Godfrey
Costume Supervisor .... Mrs. Sadie John |
FOR WORTHING CORPORATION :
Director of Entertainment & Publicity: ROBERT S. BATTERSBY, F.I.M.Ent., M.I.A.M.A.
Pavilion Manager : Peter Bland   Stage Manager : Bert Sarney

more. When Fellows left Eastbourne, Sandy took over the reins and a new partnership was forged, almost by accident. It would prove very successful.

Norman Meadow, who had come to live in Eastbourne just after the war, applied for a job in Walter Fellows's show as stage manager. One night, Sandy was doing a sketch and there was nobody free in the show to feed him. Norman volunteered and Sandy was so pleased with the result that he asked Fellows if Norman could join the show working on-stage instead of behind the scenes. This was agreed, and when Sandy started his own summer shows — called *Starlight* — in the mid-1950s, Norman became part of the management team. Indeed, Norman and Sandy stayed together until the shows finished in 1970, when the Pier Theatre was burnt down by an arsonist.

Above: The 'Fol-de-Rols' at Worthing Pier Pavilion in 1967, promising 'New Fun! New Faces! New Airs! New Graces!'

Norman was a marvellous feed and played a great part in the success and popularity of Sandy's shows. Sometimes a comedian's feed does not always get the recognition he deserves, but when a good partnership develops, he is worth his weight in gold.

After *Starlight* finished Sandy toured in various variety shows, at home and abroad, and gave some memorable television programmes with his ventriloquist doll that was always falling apart — great stuff. Norman Meadow, meanwhile, became manager of the Pier, bringing all his experience and expertise to his new job. He laid a lot of the foundations for the pier's present success, which is

Sandy Powell.

there for all to see. It is one of Eastbourne's most popular attractions.

The 'Fol-de-Rols' carried on at the Winter Gardens, and I can remember being part of the company in 1958, along with Jack Tripp, Allen Christie, Joy Jackley and Patricia Lambert. We played to incredible audiences — about 1,500 people a night — and it was while there that I heard I was going to join the cast of radio's *Beyond Our Ken*. I was engaged for six episodes which were extended to eight and a half years. This included the follow-on show *Round the Horne*.

One of our great moments at Eastbourne came one

night when we had a call from the nearby Hippodrome Theatre, informing us that the principal comedian in the show *Gaytime* had just been engaged to take over the role of compère for TV's *Sunday Night at the London Palladium* — it was Bruce Forsyth. That was rather like winning the pools, and everyone wanted to celebrate his much deserved good fortune.

I had first seen Bruce in 1956 when my wife and I were doing a season down in Newquay, in deepest Cornwall. Someone had told us we should try and see this terrific performer in his show at Babbacombe, just outside Torquay in south Devon. So we all decided to hire a coach and make the trip to Babbacombe and see his Sunday show. It was called *Gaytime* and was so entertaining. Bruce did a 'give-away' spot, getting members of the audience up on stage with hilarious results, and also showed his versatility with his singing and dancing and piano playing. We were completely won over, so you can imagine how pleased we were two years later when we heard his good news.

The Devonshire Park Theatre was going great guns and has done since the 1970s. I have played there in various productions, one of them with Arthur Lowe, which was a delight of course, and with Mollie Sugden, and in my Cousin Michael's hilarious comedy *Don't Just Lie There, Say Something!*

I have also watched my son in several plays there, and particularly remember one, when he acted alongside a particular favourite of mine, Brian Murphy. I have had some laughs with Brian on-stage I can tell you, particularly while on tour in Canada.

The New Congress Theatre opened in 1963, and started to take all the big star name productions, but that opening season was given to who else but the 'Fol-de-Rols'. Quite rightly too. They had always been successful at Eastbourne and part of the scene. The New Congress had all the amenities of a modern theatre and became the flagship of Eastbourne's entertainment programme.

One man who has now made his home in Eastbourne and often appears there for a season is Russ Conway. He did tell me, however, that he still has a soft spot for St Anne's near Blackpool, where he did his very first summer season in a show called *Let's Be Gay*, and we both agreed it would be difficult to use that title

Left: Two rascals together in one show!

Sea front at Eastbourne.

today! Strangely enough a lot of shows in the past had 'gay' in their titles, when all it meant was jollity, laughter and happiness. I'm afraid our politically correct lot might object today. We will meet up again with Russ in other resorts. He's played a lot of them.

One little thought about a dear gentleman who ran many repertory companies, notably the 'Penguin Players', at the Little Theatre on the Leas at **Folkestone** and **Bexhill-on-Sea**. His name was Arthur Brough and when he retired from the theatre, he imagined he would spend his leisure time just like everyone else did, pottering about meeting old friends and swapping yarns about the theatre. But then along came a television series that brought Arthur Brough a new career in front of a bigger audience worldwide. The series, one of the BBC's top situation comedy successes, was *Are You Being Served*. It was co-written and produced by my old friend David Croft. It has a cult following in America and is regularly watched all over Europe, Australia and New Zealand. It's a funny old business — just when you think it's the pipe and slippers for you in front of the fire, something else happens!

Some **Thanet** summer resorts still had a good following for the entertainment on offer well into the 1960s. Shows like the 'Fol-de-Rols', Clarkson Rose's 'Twinkle', Betty Lunn's 'Bouquests', in which I played for two seasons at Bognor, Hedley Claxton's *Gaytime*, John Berryman's 'Evening Stars', Brandon and Pounds' 'Out of the Blue', Frank Adey's 'Ocean Revue' at Clacton, and Sandy Powell's 'Starlight' with its huge following at Eastbourne.

In the 1950s there was no sign, at least in the early part of the decade, that the small summer show was heading for its demise. Cecil Johnson was packing in the deckchair customers, sometimes 2,000 a performance, alfresco style. He later repeated the success at Eastbourne's Redoubt, again alfresco entertainment. Also successful was Bill Fraser and Bob O'Connor's *Between Ourselves* at Westgate and later at Lowestoft. After *Between Ourselves* finished at Westgate, comedian Clifford Hensley took over the Pavilion there with his fine little summer revue, 'Gaiety at Eight', for several seasons.

Dickie Henderson.

All the performers who played in this sort of small summer show have a great regard for a period in their lives that was really an apprenticeship for what was to become their profession in the future. Pamela Cundell told me that:

'Working in the open air at Cliftonville taught you to use your voice in the best possible way and to make yourself heard distinctly without shouting. You had to communicate with the audience as if you were performing to just one person This stood you in good stead for the medium of television.'

Pamela Cundell has certainly had a wonderful career in musicals, straight plays and, of course, television. She was always in top form in *Dad's Army*, particularly in the very last episode when she married Corporal Jones, quite a marvellous performance from her and Arthur Lowe in the scenes they had together.

A view from the audience was expressed to me by Max Tyler, the British Music Hall Society historian, on his visits to the Oval at Cliftonville:

'On my first visit to the Oval at Cliftonville just after the war, you sat in that huge audience in the open air but you felt that the performers were playing just to you, it is a gift some people have. We would meet the artistes afterwards and shake hands with them and you felt you were friends, and of course that is exactly what they wanted you to feel. There was Cecil Johnson, the proprietor, and Fred Gwynne, the principal comedian, and just four or five other artistes, all very professional.'

Tyler came to love the concert party shows and travelled all over the place and listened to stories about the players at the seaside.

When Elsie and Doris Waters were at the Southwold Pavilion, the public had to walk through the pavilion even when there was a show on to catch the steamers that plied round the coast on sight-seeing trips. Apparently at Southwold there were no ladies lavatories for the artistes. When one of the pianists was asked about this while he

was sitting at the piano ready to start the show, he just said, without looking up, 'You can use ours. Start the overture Ethel (or whatever was the name of the other pianist),' as if the need of a toilet were not going to hold up his usual activity of crashing into the overture at the start of the show. He also said, in his droll way, one night just before the start of the show, 'Do you realise that every night of the week at about this time 300 pianos are about to strike up a particular opening chorus all round the seaside resorts.'

The 'Poppies' company was playing on the pier at Teignmouth in South Devon and the one and only toilet was at the back of the stage, but the company manager would not let anyone use it while the show was on as the flush made such a noise. One night one of the girl dancers, just had to go. She was severely reprimanded afterwards with the words, 'You know the rules, remember you're a poppy.'

Wilby Lunn, the producer of the 'Bouquets' and Will

Left: The Pier and Lower Promenade, Eastbourne.

Right: Souvenir programme for 'Starlight Rendezvous' at the De La Warr Pavilion, Bexhill-on-Sea.

Left and Below: Norman Wisdom then . . . and now.

sible, you could book up for their last night at the end of the season, which would be a request night, when they presented the most popular items from their season. All the artistes would have a present or two handed up to them at the end of the show as farewell gifts from the residents.

'Then you'd wait for the thanks of the chairman and the council to hear whether the show would be coming back the following year and whether any of the artistes would be returning with it.'

Progress of course occurs in all walks of life, but what lovely memories the small and sometimes not so small concert parties had given to a lot of people. At a much later date Norman Wisdom was playing at **Margate** and

Seymour's 'Bubbles', always said it was just as important to engage artistes who were nice people as it was for their talent. Max Tyler went on to say:

'It was always a treat to meet the artistes after the show, perhaps in the pier bar where you would have a drink with them and then walk back along the pier with its twinkling lights, after another jolly evening amongst those you could call friends. The artistes had enjoyed the show as well and it felt as if we had all been part of the company on stage. This was what summer concert parties were all about.

'Sometimes, if you stayed in a resort for more than a few days, you would meet one or two of the cast in the local cafe and join them for a cup of coffee. If it was pos-

Right: A very early appearance of the Cardiff Bay lassie Shirley Bassey. I happened to see this show, and what an impact she made!

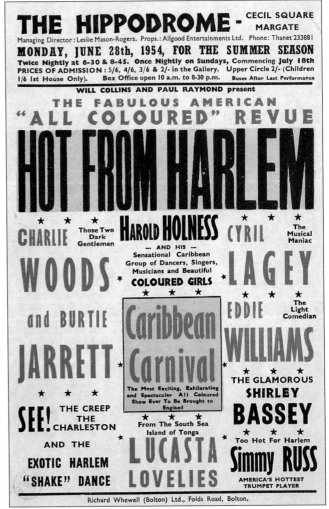

THE HIPPODROME - CECIL SQUARE MARGATE

Managing Director : Leslie Mason-Rogers. Props. : Allgood Entertainments Ltd. Phone: Thanet 23388I

MONDAY, JUNE 28th, 1954, FOR THE SUMMER SEASON

Twice Nightly at 6-30 & 8-45. Once Nightly on Sundays, Commencing July 18th
PRICES OF ADMISSION : 5/6, 4/6, 3/6 & 2/- in the Gallery. Upper Circle 2/- (Children 1/6 1st House Only). Box Office open 10 a.m. to 8-30 p.m. Buses After Last Performance

WILL COLLINS AND PAUL RAYMOND present

THE FABULOUS AMERICAN
"ALL COLOURED" REVUE

HOT FROM HARLEM

CHARLIE Those Two Dark Gentlemen HAROLD HOLNESS CYRIL The Musical Maniac

— AND HIS —
Sensational Caribbean Group of Dancers, Singers, Musicians and Beautiful COLOURED GIRLS

WOODS LAGEY

and BURTIE Caribbean Carnival EDDIE The Light Comedian

JARRETT WILLIAMS

The Most Exciting, Exhilarating and Spectacular All Coloured Show Ever To Be Brought to England

THE GLAMOROUS SHIRLEY

SEE! THE CREEP THE CHARLESTON From The South Sea Island of Tonga BASSEY

AND THE EXOTIC HARLEM "SHAKE" DANCE LUCASTA LOVELIES Too Hot For Harlem Simmy RUSS
AMERICA'S HOTTEST TRUMPET PLAYER

Richard Whewell (Bolton) Ltd., Folds Road, Bolton.

A young Bill Maynard
(Greengrass from TV's *Heartbeat*).

I would like to quote from the programme for his visit. It says it all about this amazing performer:
'We are proud to have Norman at Margate. He has succeeded in everything, theatre, films, television, ice shows, cabaret and music hall. He has played all over the world, and scored immense triumphs. In America he starred on Broadway in *Walking Happy* for which he won two awards and was nominated for the best supporting actor in the film *The Night They Raided Minskey's*. His first starring role for the British Rank Organisation was in *Trouble in Store* for which he won an Academy Award. He has also appeared in several Royal Variety Performances. His *Turn Again Whittington* pantomime at the London Palladium was a huge success and proved the biggest box office draw ever at that time. His television shows for ATV included *Nobody is Norman* and *A Little Bit of Wisdom*.'

There is little I can say after that except that, having worked with him in some of his early TV appearances, I found him a delightfully friendly fellow. I asked him one

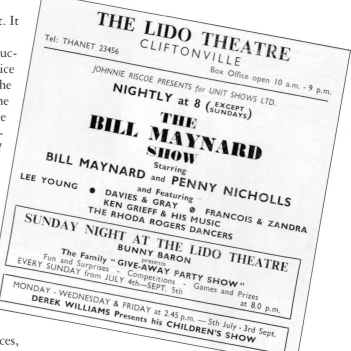

THE PROVIDERS
Producers of big shows were always on the lookout for new and interesting talent and it was often the agent's job to find it. Not content to sit in their offices and let the artistes come to them, they combed the summer resorts and such like hoping to find that all too elusive performer with star potential.

One such enterprising and far-sighted man was Richard Stone (Colonel Stone from Chapter Two) who had set up an agency with a partner immediately after the war and had a very keen eye for talent.

He spotted Benny Hill in a show at Margate and with a handshake immediately put him on his books. Benny was a feed in that show to comedian Reg Varney, who was already an established performer and went on to star in the successful *On the Buses* on TV and the film spin-off. Reg Varney was a wonderful asset to any show with his warm sense of humour and great rapport with his audience. It is not perhaps widely known that, apart from being a good comedy actor, Reg is also a very fine pianist.

Richard Stone guided Benny Hill through those first important years on the road to stardom. Benny became something of an institution, particularly in

the United States where he still has an enormous and enthusiastic following.

Stone also spotted the newly emerging talents of Bill Maynard and Terry Scott, and guided their early careers. Other artistes in the Stone stable were Norman Vaughn, Billy Burden and Felix Bowness, and many top actors and actresses.

He also presented many summer revues which were produced and directed by two other clients of his, David Croft and Ian Carmichael.

I myself have been looked after by Richard and his partners since 1964 (apart from a short break at the beginning of the 1970s) and I consider myself fortunate in that respect, as I am sure I must have forced myself on him initially. A good move, don't you think?

Richard is now retired and lives on the coast where he tends his lobster pots, and in the winter months travels the world quite happily with his wife Sara on what appear to be banana boats. They both find the time to visit their son and grandchildren in America.

The agency is now run very successfully by a wonderful team of ladies and they handle a number of very high-flyers in the business.

Dickie Henderson headlining at the Cliffs Pavilion, Southend-on-Sea.

Left: That's what we all like to see — House Full! One of the big present day success stories — the West Cliff Theatre, Clacton. In the centre, Don Maclean, to his left Beryl and Tom Plummer and company.

Hudd (of which the local critic headlined his newspaper comments of the show, 'A typhoon named Hudd hits the Ocean Revue'). Other super performers during Adey's career at the Ocean Room were Don Smoothey, Gwen Overton and Clive Stock, Billy Burden and Bryan Burdon (no relation). After Frank Adey retired, the big TV names were booked for the shows, and numerous comedians did a season there — such as Harry Worth, Leslie Crowther, Dickie Henderson and Arthur Askey.

By 1977 it seemed obvious that the type of holidaymaker who had previously gone to Clacton for their summer holiday had changed their habits. They were leaving the seaside to the day trippers because they had started to go abroad or to Butlin's Holiday Camp, just off the front at Clacton. The audiences for the big shows began to drop.

However, along came Francis Golightly, a man who loved the family atmosphere of seaside summer shows. He took over the West Cliff Theatre and, along with other folk and builders, proceeded to restore and modernise it. Not knowing whether he would be able to draw the crowds was a big gamble. Someone said to him, 'Do you realise they are getting big names at the Ocean Pavilion now, do you think you can compete with that?'

They didn't have to wait too long to see that the gamble had worked. Just as at Cromer, the success came without big names but with good working pros. Golightly went for glamour and big production numbers; from the word go, the audiences came back to West Cliff and have remained faithful to it. The trend, I know, will continue as it now has a firmly established reputation.

What is very important is that artistes, such as Don Maclean, Alan Randal, Norman Collier, Don Smoothey, Dorothy Wayne and Peter Goodright have all loved playing there. Francis Golightly also unearthed the talents of stars Ruthie Henshall, Gary Wilmot and others. Golightly would be the first to admit that he has had

day how the Gump character came about, with tight suit, funny cap and silly walk. He told me it happened at Scarborough when he was in a summer show there. The conjuror David Nixon was in the show and he wanted a stooge to come up from the audience and help him with a trick, then muck it all up, after which he could put it all back together properly. Norman, having agreed, decided to go out and buy a funny suit and cap, so that he really would look a 'gump' when he got on stage. The whole thing was an immediate success and from that moment on Norman was the 'Gump'.

I have to tell you that even now, in his 80s, he can still do the stage falls and somersaults, and I bet if you put a set of drums in front of him he could still do a very good drum solo — once part of his act. I remember a wonderful *Sunday Night at the Palladium* during a technicians' strike when he and Bruce Forsyth carried the evening with some great comedy. I am proud and privileged to call the 'Gump' my friend.

After World War II the 'Ocean Revue' in the Pavilion at **Clacton** continued where it had left off in 1939, again under the direction of Frank Adey until his retirement in 1971. In that time he fostered the careers of many young artistes who went on to bigger things, such as Tony Hancock, Billy Dainty, Felix Bowness, Ted Rogers, Roy

Bernie Clifton and that ostrich.

tremendous support from the local district council and residents of Clacton-on-Sea.

I haven't yet seen one of his productions, but I certainly will this summer, and everyone who has says they are wonderful. Francis has been enticed on more than one occasion to produce at other resorts, but he is quite happy to concentrate on Clacton. In 1999 his top team will include Bernie Clifton and his huge ostrich, and Alan Randall, who does a marvellous impression of George Formby, complete with ukelele.

In fact Randall starred in a play of Formby's life with Dorothy Wayne. Another favourite at the West Cliff Theatre, comedian Don Smoothey, who has worked a lot for Francis says he's great to be with.

I must thank Vince and Rita Starr, who have also worked at the West Cliff, for introducing me to Golightly. He is obviously a man of the theatre.

The Sparrow's Nest Theatre in **Lowestoft** was the venue for Hedley Claxton's *Gaytime* in 1949 and through into the 1950s. Phil Burn then took over the date with his summer show in 1954 and 1955. Bernie Clifton and his Ostrich first went to the 'Nest' in 1977, and although Bernie has played at practically every resort in the country, he has a particular affection for Lowestoft. It was his first seaside summer show and once he'd settled into the routine of rehearsals and performances, the personality of the young eccentric practical joker took

Above: One of Lowestoft's biggest successes: Bill Fraser became the lynch pin of television's *Bootsie and Snudge*.

that time on the ladies were pretty wary of him and no wonder! (The pig's head will appear again on the Isle of Wight.) Bernie must have got his eccentricity from his parents, who did a 'Romany' act on the music halls. He recalls that his father wore a turban and his mother went round the audience selling pegs! This was so successful they kept it in the act.

He also told me that when he was first starting in the business his name on the posters was very tiny and so low down that the little dogs used to cock their hind legs and give their opinion in no uncertain way.

I personally have an affection for the nearby **Gorleston** Pavilion. After the war Harry and Marjorie Ristori took the Pavilion over and presented *Hilarity*, and in 1954 Henry Lutman arrived with his show *Summertime*. This was very successful and he returned in 1955. I joined the company that year and it was my very first summer season show.

I don't wish to go into too many details of my first experiences in show business — I've covered them elsewhere. Suffice to say that I was a very raw recruit and probably not very good. I often wonder how I came to be given the job. However, I was not being paid a great deal and I fitted the costumes! I believe Henry Lutman liked me as a person and hoped I would fit into his little family show — something that is very important when a small company has to pull together.

I remember it was a wonderful summer with beautiful weather. I

over. For instance, on one occasion, two of the girls in the company were a bit 'uppish' and to pull them down a peg or two, Bernie bought a pig's head from the local butcher and placed it in the girls' lavatory. One can only imagine the shrieks and screams when it was discovered! From

played tennis, and cricket and swam during the day, but at night on stage there were some very nervous moments for me because I had very little material and hardly any talent to offer. However, thanks to the generous help from my fellow artistes who helped to lick me into shape, I

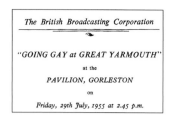

The British Broadcasting Corporation

"GOING GAY at GREAT YARMOUTH"
at the
PAVILION, GORLESTON
on
Friday, 29th July, 1955 at 2.45 p.m.

Going Gay at Great Yarmouth.

Top: A great day for us at the Pavilion. Cast includes the author, Cliff Hersley, and the 'Gorleston Lovelies'.

Above: The Beverleys, Tommy Trinder, Charlie Chester, Billy Whittaker and Ronnie Ronalde.

Below: Those gals again.

shall always remember the season of 1955 as the jumping-off point for anything I might have done since. Oh, and by the way, I met my wife Marion in that show, and that was nearly 45 years ago.

I had made a lot of friends while at the Pavilion, and from the other shows at the theatres in nearby Great Yarmouth, people such as the Beverley Sisters, Charlie Chester, Tommy Trinder, Billy Whittaker and Mimi Law, Ronnie Ronalde and Jack Jay. The Pavilion has gone through many changes in the past, but is now leased to Kevin Lynch and Stuart Durrant, who put on all sorts of entertainment, such as pantomime, summer shows, olde tyme music hall and concerts of every description. Long may they reign!

That lovely man, Jimmy Cricket, says he remembers his first summer season was on the Wellington Pier, **Great Yarmouth**, in 1982:

'It was a happy show with a lovely cast and I came to think there was something special about Pier entertainment.

'The promoter was an Irishman called Dick Condon, a genial guy with a twinkle in his eye and a nice line in blarney. He previously had built up the Theatre Royal in Norwich into one of the best venues in the country and even now the Pier Theatre at Cromer is a monument to his skills as an entrepreneur.

'You would be walking down the pier to the theatre and if the show was doing good business it was also good for the stall holders.

'The hoop-la games, throwing darts at playing cards, the fortune teller all gave you a smile and a cheery greeting because the show was helping their business. Dick Condon had a great idea, letting the pensioners and young children in for only a pound. Of course they used to spread the word and we did a smashing season that year at Yarmouth.'

Jimmy went on to play many resorts around our coasts, including on several occasions, Blackpool:

'Once, when I was playing on the South Pier, the show went on to October to coincide with the illuminations. It was terribly cold and members of the   audience were all wrapped in thick overcoats and scarves. Halfway through my act a man in the front row jumped up and said, "Will somebody open the doors and let the heat in!"'

The Beverley Sisters.

An extraordinary incident happened when Jimmy was playing at the Grand Theatre in the town:

'A man died in the third row, while I was on stage. The St John's Ambulance man was quickly on the spot but didn't believe the man was really dead He kept reassuring the man's wife that he was only pretending The wife insisted her husband had "snuffed it". The ambulance man was finally convinced and said sadly, "Oh dear, I've only ever done bandages and fainting."'

One night, playing on one of the piers, the gales were so strong that he announced to the audience 'hold tight to your seats, we'll be entering the Bay of Biscay in 20 minutes!' I'll bet that got a woofer (a good laugh). Jimmy says he still has a great affection for Great Yarmouth, which gave him such a happy start to his summer show experiences.

I had nearly four years working with Jimmy, along with Peter Goodwright, Noreen Kershaw, writer Eddie Braben and producer Mike Craig on *Jimmy's Cricket Team* for BBC radio, a delightful experience.

Another amusing incident during a season at Great Yarmouth happened to the lovely Beverley Sisters. The 'Bevs', as they are affectionately known, were doing a season there in the mid-1960s and they had their families with them. Joy's husband, the marvellous Wolves and England football captain, the late Billy Wright, used to join them at weekends.

Once, the girls were asked to do some publicity for their show and were put in an open carriage and driven by a team of horses up and down the sea front. The horses unfortunately had been given too much breakfast and this resulted in a trail on the road behind them. The girls intimated to the coach driver that they were in the process of making some nice gardens at their new houses back in London, and the horse-droppings were just what they needed for the roses! The driver said there was no problem. He would collect it and bag it up for them.

When Billy Wright went back to London after the weekend, the bags were duly stowed in the boot of his car. He was very busy during the following week, not least of his engagements being to have lunch with the Queen at Buckingham Palace.

The following weekend he went back again to Yarmouth and the girls said they had some more bags of manure for him to take home. When they opened the boot of his car, they found the original bags were still in there. He had been travelling around all week with them,

Above: . . . and there's more — Jimmy Cricket.

Right: A poster for the Pavilion Theatre, Yarmouth from 1952.

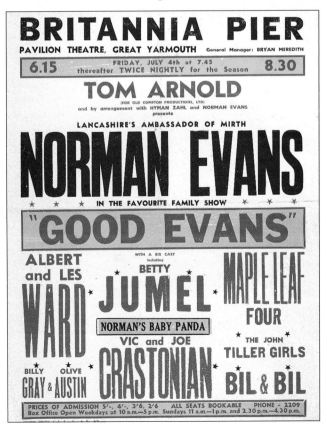

Britannia Pier, Yarmouth in its heyday.

completely oblivious, what with the visit to the palace and the journeys to and fro and the hot weather. One can only imagine what sort of smell greeted them! I wonder if the other drivers gave Billy any funny looks when they got near his car. It certainly did their gardens a bit of good, they're lovely — fertilizer by Royal Appointment!

I'm sure other pros have stories to tell about their seasons at the various venues in that bustling seaside resort on Norfolk's east coast. I have a story of coincidence to relate about the Marina Bandstand, on the front, not far from the Wellington Pier. The show presented there featured Neville Bishop and his band, and included a fine compère and raconteur, Bob Andrews, and some very good vocalists. It was great entertainment and extremely popular.

I met up with Neville Bishop on several occasions in 1955 and 15 years or so later, when I arrived in Thetford (a lovely historic country town between Newmarket and Norwich) to film some episodes of *Dad's Army* with the television crew, I met a charming lady who ran one of the hotels in the town. Over a drink she said to me, 'I think you knew my late husband Neville, he ran the band shows on the front at Yarmouth in the 1950s' — it's a small world! Jean Bishop carried on at the Anchor Hotel after Neville died and a lot of the *Dad's Army* cast and technicians stayed there over a period of nine years: Jean was the perfect hostess.

Yarmouth today has obviously changed as much as other resorts have, but the list of top line artistes that have played the two piers, Jack Jay's Windmill Theatre and other venues in the town, is as long as your arm. The days when the piers were used by pierrot proprietors, such as Walter Paskin, Will Catlin, Reg Maddox, then Dick Condon and others, are part of history and it was thought that they would never be repeated.

Above: Bruce Forsyth well on his way up, showing at Wellington Pier Theatre, 1961.

However, hey presto, in the 1990s an entertainer and proprietor arrived on the scene to take over Wellington Pier. It was Jim Davidson, of TV fame. Jim, however, is not just a pretty face on our TV screens, he has vision and ambitious plans for the Wellington. On a personal note, Jim is very generous with his free time, and there are many charitable causes that have reason to be grateful for this.

The Pier Pavilion theatre at **Cromer** started off with a few problems after the war. Cromer Council invited Brandon and Pounds to bring their 'Out of the Blue' Company to the Pier Pavilion, but huge gales demolished the building and wrecked that part of the pier. Rebuilding took place and it opened again in 1955 with Wilby Lunn's 'Bouquets' who stayed for some time until they were replaced by Eric Ross's 'Dazzle' and then again 'Out of the Blue'.

In 1978 alterations took place, slightly reducing the seating capacity but providing extra facilities, a cafe bar

Below and Right:
Cromer Pier and Pavilion then, and . . . now.

and new toilets. At the same time, the North Norfolk District Council went into partnership with Dick Condon Management, who had done a marvellous job revitalising the Theatre Royal, Norwich, where Dick Condon was based. This was a great move, because there was no doubt that the theatre had to become much more of a summer revue date if it was to survive. The concert parties had been good, but they lacked the money for the big productions, lavish costumes and attractive headliners needed for success.

The combination of council money and Condon's expertise reaped rewards and the venture gained the success it deserved — and continues to do so. The artistes involved over the years have not been the really big show business names you might expect, but they were all really good professionals who knew their job, people like Ken Joy, Don Smoothey, Milligan and Nesbit, Denny Willis, Dorothy Wayne, Michelle Summers, Syd Wright, Denis Lotis, Gordon and Bunny Jay, and Rosemary Squires and the Simmons Brothers for four seasons (three of them consecutively). Much of the success of the shows is due to director and choreographer Robert Marlow. Robert has a wealth of experience as a performer in summer shows and as a pantomime producer. This quiet chap has been in charge of the Pier Theatre's productions since 1983.

I have mentioned the Simmons Brothers again because not only have I seen them in three of their recent years at Cromer, but I have also done pantomime with them. They are a wonderful comedy duo and I put them in the same league as Morecambe and Wise, and Jewel and Warns. They need just one good television series to lift their name to the top rung of the ladder. They never stop working in concerts, supporting stars like Max Bygraves and Norman Wisdom, and Keith (he's the silly one) writes pantomimes that are played all over the country with the big star names.

The theatre also presents other shows during the year, including many one-night stands with top names. Ken Dodd once said to me that there are only two really good summer shows left in the country that do not have big names at the top of their programmes but still manage to bring in the families. One is Cromer and the other one is — be patient, wait and see!

Scarborough moved into the second half of the century with several long-running sequences of entertainments. In the 1950s and 1960s the 'Dazzle' revues were at the Spa Theatre, firstly under the management of the experienced Eric Ross, and then the tradition was carried on by his daughter Brenda.

At the Spa Grand Hall, Max Jaffa and his orchestra were resident every summer for 27 years from 1960 onwards. Max Jaffa was a phenomenon. He had a marvellous following thanks to his radio and television broadcasts, and the Max Jaffa Trio could have worked 24 hours a day had they wanted, such was their popularity. The Trio was made up of Max, Jack Byfield at the piano and

Roy Hudd — going mad as usual at the Floral Hall, Scarborough in 1968!

PROGRAMME ONE SHILLING

The BLACK and WHITE Minstrel Show

Based on the popular B.B.C T.V Series

cellist Reginald Kilby — all great musicians. Max and the boys will be remembered for radio's 'Grand Hotel' and many television appearances.

Max's wife, Jean Grayston, was already established as a fine singer and knew Scarborough well, having played there with Eugene Pini and Charles Shadwell, and productions of *King's Rhapsody* and *South Pacific*.

Early in the 1990s I spent two delightful days with Max and Jean and one of their daughters. We were all on a book signing tour of the north of England. Max signed a copy of his autobiography — the reason for his place on the trip — 'For Bill, what a great treat to meet and laugh with you, Max'. That's one of the nicest dedications I've seen in a book. If you have never read Max's autobiography do try to get hold of a copy, it is one of the best I've ever read.

The other great story from Scarborough must surely be the beginning of the 'Black and White Minstrels'. They made their debut at the Futurist Theatre and became an immediate success, with the television series following. This established the Minstrels as one of the most popular musical/variety programmes ever. The stage production not only made household names of the principal singers but the comedy talents of people like Leslie Crowther and Stan Stennet were brought before a wider public. It was a huge triumph for conductor George Mitchell, TV director George Inns, and overall stage producer, Robert Luff.

I have talked about many of the star names and comedians who have played the resort, but a few still linger in the memory of the faithful **Blackpool** audiences. Take, for example, Lancastrian Ken Platt, with that marvellous droll way of his, and the shy smile, when he would say on his entrance, with perfect timing, 'I won't take me coat off, I'm not stopping'. He was not only a big radio star in the 1950s and 1960s, but was a wonderful pantomime performer as well.

Max Wall began his impression of a mad concert pianist in Blackpool when he was a corporal in the RAF, entertaining his fellow servicemen. His Professor Wallofski was a joy to watch, and thank goodness there is television footage available for all to see. I remember doing a week's variety in Sunderland with Max, not perhaps the best place for an eccentric British comedian to play, but Max went through his whole routine twice nightly, giving one hundred per cent while he tried to coax a few laughs from the audience. I was enthralled watching from the wings. One day I told him I was going to buy a pair of shoes, he said, 'I'll come with you.' I bought my shoes and Max said to the young lady assistant 'Have you got those in size 12?'. Now Max had very small feet, and he tried on one of the shoes, which of course was miles too big. He said to the lady, 'Oh no, they'll fall off all over the High Street.' It was difficult for me to keep a straight face.

One of the most lovable of our comedians was Les Dawson, who not only eventually made his home at St Anne's, but was playing the night spots, small and large, in and around Blackpool well before he moved into the big time. He was a huge favourite, playing most of the theatres there. His work was very varied and he was as comfortable in stage plays at the Grand as he was doing his hilarious 'stand-up' routines. He had this wonderful comic way with words, which he used to great effect as a

Moreton Fraser's Harmonica Gang.

writer — another string to his bow, and he had several books published. He had a long and successful career in television, with his own series and as host in the game show *Blankety Blank*. He made several appearances in Royal Variety performances and was a great favourite on such occasions.

Other well known names to have played regularly around Blackpool include Charlie Drake, who played in the resort at an early stage in his career, and Tommy Cooper, who amazed his audiences with his magic tricks that always went wrong, followed by that maniacal laugh. Tony Hancock appeared at the Palace and the Opera House but I don't think he found Blackpool quite his cup of tea.

Roy Castle was not just a great performer. Had he been in American Vaudeville, I think he would have enjoyed success in film and stage, and his talent given greater opportunity. Be that as it may, he has left a great legacy of TV footage for us to enjoy and remember with affection. As early as 1948 he was in the concert party 'Happiness Ahead' at Cleveleys, the town where he was brought up. Roy was once part of the wonderful Jimmy James stage act. (Who can ever forget 'The Lion in the Box'?), and then blossomed out into a marvellous variety and cabaret performer. He played several seasons in Blackpool and was a great friend of another son of the town, agent and producer Norman Teal.

Roy was equally at home in his long running T.V. series *Record Breakers*. When he became ill at a comparatively early age, he campaigned and took in a national tour to raise funds for a special unit in Liverpool, which hopefully can deal with the illness that finally took away from us the talent that was Roy Castle.

Peter Goodwright has brought his comedy talent and amazing range of voices and impressions to the resort on many occasions, and his ability as an actor in comedy plays to Blackpool on several occasions. It is a delightful experience to work with him.

A little known comedian outside Blackpool was Jimmy Edmunson. He could communicate with his audience very quickly, a great asset for a performer. He called himself 'Also on the Bill', a position he

often occupied on variety bills, supporting the big star names. In between jobs he worked as a washer-up in Woolworth's cafeteria, the Fleetwood Fish Market and painting scenery at one of Blackpool's theatres.

I worked with Jimmy at London's Windmill Theatre, when he had a comedy feed with him, Peter Elliott, who you will meet later in the book. Jim was a delight to work with, he never grumbled, even through adversity. He spent the last 15 years of his life happily employed as the stage-door keeper at the Orchard Theatre, Dartford, where he said he was just happy to be with the pros. He wrote a book of his life, which has never been published. I'm sure it contains some wonderful gems of Edmundson humour and a few moments of hardship too.

Above Left: The theatre production of the popular television show.

Right: A Headley Clayton production.

A Jimmy Brennan production in Blackpool.

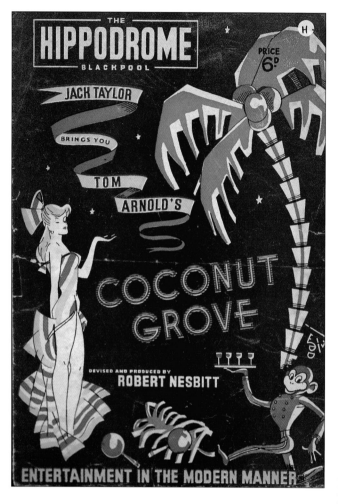

What about Hylda Baker, with her tall female-impersonator feed 'Cynthia', who just stood there and looked, and was always on the receiving end of Hylda's 'She knows you know!' and 'Be soon'. One cannot explain in print the comedy that was extracted from these two phrases. If you have a chance to see Jean Fergusson's one-woman show *The Story of Hylda Baker*, make sure you watch it, as it is a brilliant re-creation of this amazing little woman's life and work in the theatre.

Dora Bryan is another of the many artistes who have enjoyed playing Blackpool. Her career spans many years, and during it she has played every West End theatre and touring date in a very long list of comedies, musicals, pantomines and serious drama. Her television and film credits are diverse and have established Dora as one of our finest actresses. She told me:

'I have really loved my seasons in Blackpool, it's a wonderful place to work in — all those theatres, the Tower Ballroom, and clubs and pubs, all for us to entertain in and be entertained. When I was a little girl in Oldham where I lived, I never thought I'd have top billing at the Opera House and Queens Theatre in Blackpool. I was very thrilled to be working with the great singer and cabaret artiste Joan Savage, because when I was very young I saw her at the Tower Ballroom where she was in a troupe of child dancers.'

I wonder how well Dora remembers her first summer season as a very young dancer in Walter Paskins 'Come to the Show' in the late 1930s, at the Wellington Pier, Great Yarmouth. She couldn't have started in a more glamorous production, as Paskins's shows were always so well dressed and presented. If I'd known Dora really well (I only met her briefly a couple of times) I would love to have talked cricket with her husband, Bill Lawton, who was a professional cricketer in his hey-day.

It may not be widely known but many American stars have appeared in Blackpool over the years. Singer and film star Alan Jones (remember *The Donkey Serenade?*, perhaps more famous now as the father of singer Jack Jones), Duke Ellington with his orchestra, Count Basie and his band, Howard Keel, Johnny Ray, Frankie Laine and 'Old Blue Eyes' himself, Frank Sinatra.

The British contingent included the wonderful Shirley Bassey, many, many times; Dickie Valentine, Joan Regan, Russ Conway, Cliff Richard with and without the Shadows, Eve Bosell, the Beatles, the Beverley Sisters, Gracie Fields, Eddie Calver with his golden trumpet and the haunting *Oh, Mein Papa*, George Formby, Gerry Marsden and the Pacemakers with the great song *Ferry Cross the Mersey*; Tom Jones and Englebert Humperdink have also brought their great talents to Blackpool.

I am going to stick my neck out and say that no other resort has played host to so many star musicians. The list of actors and actresses who have graced the stage of the Grand Theatre is quite amazing: Michael Denison and Dulcie Gray, Sybil Thorndike, Michael Redgrave and his daughter Vanessa, Dame Edith Evans, Noel Coward, Richard Attenborough, Antony Quale, Margaret Rutherford, Anna Neagle, Peggy Ashcroft, and as comedian Jimmy Cricket would say *'And there's more!'*

I wonder how many people realise that the television glove puppet 'Sooty' was discovered in Blackpool. Harry

Joan Regan and the Clitheroe Kid, performing at Blackpool.

Corbett was walking up the North Pier when he saw the puppet on sale at a stall. He bought it for a few shillings as he thought he might amuse his children during the rainy days of the holiday. It is extraordinary to think that this little toy went on to become the most talked about puppet on television. When Harry Corbett became ill his son, Matthew, took over and now he, after a long time with 'Sooty', has passed the reins to others, who I'm sure will be taunted just as others have been by that lovable little puppet.

I am told that the seaside bathing beauty contest really started in Blackpool. I have no confirmation of this, but I'm pretty sure the Blackpool versions of those contests received more publicity and attention from the many star names who judged them than any other resort around our coasts.

If people talked about Blackpool they automatically talked about the Tower and its circus. It was amazing to watch the high wire acts, the grace and precision, the split second timing of the catching.

Above: Dora Bryan.

Above Left: A Robert Nesbitt production from 1949.

Right: What a line-up! Jean Carson, Joseph Locke, Julie Andrews, Jewel and Warriss, and company. Nowadays you might get three acts, four dancers and drums!!

There is no feeling quite like it when you are in the audience.

I would like to mention the animals that I have seen at the Tower. The care they were given at Blackpool was always confirmed by the RSPCA and the local vets. If an animal was a little off colour, the stable lads would sleep near to them so I'm not sure we should always jump to the conclusion that all performing animals have a bad time.

Another wonderful part of the Tower Circus was, of course, the clowns, where Charlie Cairoli and company were the king pins there for a long time.

I had the privilege of working with Charlie and one of his marvellous stooges, little Jimmy Cairoli. With his pale face, Jimmy took all the butts of the gags, beautifully timed and very funny. When Roy Hudd and I played the brokers men, we had a great time when we were involved in Charlie's routines that he brought to the pantomime from the circus.

Danny La Rue has a tremendous affection for Blackpool and, quite rightly, has defended Blackpool's entertainers against those who believe that the resort's shows must change in style to move smoothly into the 21st century. Danny said:

'Blackpool is Blackpool, it's fun, it's bawdy, it's noisy and

109

Mike and Bernie Winters.

its entertainers love playing there, and the audiences love them.'

Danny has a point. I must say I'm I'm surprised that one or two show managements have gone into print claiming that the 'tired' old performers of the last 15 years have no part in the future entertainment scene at the resort. These people they talk about (Ken Dodd is excluded from their list) have served Blackpool very well and hopefully will be remembered for entertaining millions of holidaymakers in their time.

Indeed, entertainment has changed in Blackpool during the last five years. Stars who felt they ought to go there but were wary that their humour might not be right for the town, have taken the plunge. One of them is Lily Savage, or more correctly Paul O'Grady, Lily's creator, who played a successful season on the North Pier in 1996. Incidentally O'Grady was born not too many miles distant from the resort in Birkenhead. Another local is John Inman, whose home town is Blackpool, and I'm pretty certain he wouldn't want to see too many changes.

The *Dad's Army* stage show was presented in Blackpool at the Opera House in 1976, and we all enjoyed the atmosphere of it. We had turned on the lights there in 1971, quite a night that was, in spite of the rain.

Writer Kenneth Shenton, describing Blackpool in 1994 said, 'statistics in every form and size abound about the resort It has 17 million visitors a year, and has more holiday beds than the whole of Portugal'.

I shall let Norman Teal have the last word about Blackpool. He is truly a son of the Fylde coast. Norman has in his time been performer and proprietor of the 'Happiness Ahead' concert party at Cleveleys, the other half of a musical double act with Roy Castle, the manager of the South Shore Pleasure Beach and a hugely successful agent in the area.

His activities as an agent have been a full-time job booking the artistes and musicians into all the main hotels in and around the resort. He is also a wonderful supporter of charitable organisations, particularly the Entertainment Artistes Benevolent Fund of which he is a Vice President. More recently he was made a Freeman of the City of London. I attended the ceremony and the lunch afterwards with his family and I know this shy, delightful man was really proud to receive that honour.

Norman says about Blackpool:

'It's been my home and work place for 60 years and I wouldn't change it for anything. I have made many friends over the years and have seen the cream of entertainment here in Blackpool and it has been a joy to have known so many of the wonderful performers. My one slight regret is that you don't get the really eccentric characters in our business now: Frank Randle, Joseph Locke, Dave Morris and Flanagan and Allen's 'Crazy Gang'; my word they really were characters'

As I have said, Bernard Delfont was the driving force in bringing the big names to Blackpool after the war. A galaxy of great supporting acts, and many of them can look back on those wonderfully produced shows in that great fun town by the sea.

SOUTH PIER BLACKPOOL. PHONE: 42064.

Souvenir Programme 6d.

6-15. AND 8-30. SPECIAL SHOW SUNDAY 7·0 pm.

The Dave Morris Show

New Brighton Floral Pavilion Easter Variety show
presented by Don King in 1969.

An early post-war visitor's view of Blackpool

Bournemouth may have been more genteel, Torquay more cosmopolitan, and Scarborough more traditional, but as far as entertainment was concerned, particularly in the immediate post-World War II years, Blackpool reigned supreme, bringing colour and laughter to a war-weary nation.

The resort had everything to offer, miles and miles of golden sands, easy access by rail, with through trains from all corners of the British Isles, and an invigorating climate ('Just smell the sea air!') that would put roses in your cheeks.

There was plenty of affordable accommodation, presided over by the famous Blackpool landladies and above all, wonderful star-studded shows, lavishly presented, awash with glamour and colour, matching anything that London had to offer. There were theatres galore, three piers, the tower complex, complete with zoo, aquarium, circus, ballroom, cafes and, of course, the famous edifice, the tower itself dominating the skyline for miles around.

The pleasure beach had rides and attractions to rival anywhere in the world, not forgetting the many establishments catering for the inner man — cockle and whelk stalls, candy floss and ice cream vendors and the traditional service peculiar to most British seaside resorts, the trays of tea for the beach. No matter how much sand got into the sandwiches, there would always be the British 'cuppa' to wash it down!

The package holiday in those postwar years had yet to be invented and, in any case, the returning warrior had had his fill of 'abroad' while fighting for king and country. A week at Mrs Helliwell's Guest House, Crown Terrace, North Shore (all mod cons, baths by arrangement, good table, single gentlemen accommo-

dated) seemed nearer to heaven. Bed, breakfast and evening meal was the norm, with plenty of cafes and pubs providing a hot midday meal, fish and chips, pie and mash (mash and gravy for the baby — sixpence) and oysters and seafood for the gourmet, in the famous wine lodge on the Golden Mile.

On arrival at Central Station, the holidaymaker would be greeted with the cry 'Carry your bags sir?' an enterprising horde of small boys, complete with home-made push carts ready to take the largest suitcase on board and accompany the weary traveller to his destination for just a few pence.

Saturday was change-over day, when the thousands who had just finished their holiday were trying to board the trains just vacated by the people arriving for theirs. The streets near the station were absolutely packed with humanity, wall-to-wall; the mood, however, was one of jollity, and no one seemed to mind being squashed in the melee. It was all part of the holiday atmosphere.

The first priority after unpacking on arrival, was to book seats for all the shows. If one left it too late, all the best seats would be gone, and in order to see all the entertainment on offer in one week, careful planning was required — a different theatre every night, and perhaps a couple of matinees and a Sunday concert as well.

So after two or more hours of non-stop first class entertainment, the theatre-goers, with stars in their eyes, would step out into the night to be greeted by the wonderful Blackpool illuminations.

A ride on the top deck on one of Blackpool's unique trams, viewing the lights, with a newspaper full of fish and chips, what more could one ask for?'

Ken Dodd, has played all three, piers and every other entertainment venue there: 'The first pier I played was the Central with Jimmy Clitheroe. I returned there the following summer with Morecambe and Wise. Later I was at the South Pier with Al Read in his own show.' When Ken arrived for one particular season on one of the piers, he had a terrible bout of bronchitis, and the lady in the box office was a Mrs. Armfield, the mother of the famous footballer Jimmy Armfield. Ken recalls, The dear lady said, 'Oh, you don't sound too good, I'll make you a cup of oxo,' and from then on, for

quite a while I was drinking about 10 or 12 cups of Oxo a day!

There's something about working on a pier, that marvellous smell of the ozone as soon as you step on board. In a pier show you weren't hampered by a huge orchestra in front of you, keeping the audience at a distance. In a pier show there might only be four musicians so it was a cosy atmosphere and the audience felt part of the show.

It was a marvellous place to learn your trade. I've enjoyed playing a lot of other piers, such as Morecambe, Llandudno, Brighton, Bournemouth, Cromer,

Some of the Tiller Girls seen at Blackpool in 1948.
There were usually 16 in each show.

Left: Kenn Dodd, an extraordinary talent and someone who has a track record of making others laugh.

Eastbourne, the Britannia and Wellington at Great Yarmouth.

Oh! the lovely smell of Bloaters down by the quay. You know what a Bloater is, a kipper with a straw hat!

But I do have a soft spot for Blackpool. In 1998 I played all the Sundays at the Grand, which was wonderful, but I was sad to see that the weekday show had just one top of the bill, a couple of acts in the first half and just four dancers.

When you think of Blackpool's great shows of the past, with three or four top line artistes, wonderful scenery and costumes and a great line of dancers, often the famous Tiller Girls. Oh well, times change.

However, Blackpool will always be a marvellous centre of entertainment, even if the type of shows alter slightly to suit some of the modern trends, and I for one will continue to play the seaside, something I love doing.'

I remember meeting him when the conversation got down to the merits of TV's *Dad's Army*, and he picked out certain qualities of it, and the reasons for its success, of which I had never thought; and his appraisal of Arthur Lowe's performance was wonderful.

If I may make an appraisal of Ken Dodd, it is to say that he reminds me of two great comedians, Billy Bennett and my hero, Harry Tate. I doubt if there will ever be another Ken Dodd in my lifetime, or anyone else's for that matter.

On a slightly more serious note, I knew Ken's agent, Keith McAndrews when he was a dancing act with his wife Barbara — McAndrews and Mills. Keith could make me laugh at the drop of a hat, and I loved being in his company. I know Ken was terribly upset when Keith died fairly recently. His widow, Barbara, is still very much apart of Ken's business and my wife and I try to keep in touch with her as often as we can. She's a lovely girl.

Ken Dodd's first number one theatre date was in 1954, and his bill matter in the programme showed what sort of a road he was to travel as a comedian, it was 'Professor Yaffle Chucklebottom, Operatic Tenor and Sausage Knotter.' (How my old friend Algy More would have loved that sort of humour.) When the theatre manager saw that, he must have thought he was going to meet some sort of lunatic. When it came to inventing his now famous Diddy Men he quoted their work as being in the 'snuff quarries', and the 'Black Pudding Plantations of Knotty Ash' (the area of his actual home in a suburb of Liverpool).

Ken would be too modest to recall that after his sell out seasons in London, he was dubbed by the Press as 'a comic genius', and quite rightly so. One hasn't to forget either that he had chart-topping songs to his credit with *Tears*, *Love is like a violin* and *Happiness*. He has acted in the classics, playing Malvolio in Shakespeare's *Twelfth Night*, and very recently the court jester 'Yorick' in Kenneth Branagh's *Hamlet*. He has a finely tuned approach to comedy and is happy to discuss it with you.

It's always difficult to analyse comedy, but if it makes you laugh, it's doing its job. Doddy has the same way with words that Les Dawson had. It is not just telling funny anecdotes, it's the marvellous juxtaposition of funny phrases that actually complement a grain of truth behind them.

Finally, let Ken have his last word on Blackpool:

'It's the most bracing resort in the UK. It's nicknamed Dodge City because of its low flying seagulls. The Mayor greeted me on one occasion, shaking me warmly by the throat, then gave me the freedom of Church Street on a silver-plated bundle of firewood.

'Did you know that I was once asked to switch on the Blackpool Lights? I was highly honoured until they sent me the electricity bill.'

Thanks Ken, keep us laughing.

Marion Macleod, Blackpool, 1949.

First Season

The excitement and glamour for a very young dancer and singer is expressed here in this very descriptive piece about Marion Mcleod's first Blackpool show. She recalls with pleasure the buzz and excitement of being part of the showbusiness scene in Blackpool in the summer of 1949:

'I was fortunate to secure an engagement as dancer and understudy to the leading lady in Jack Taylor and Tom Arnold's production of "Coconut Grove" at the Hippodrome Theatre (the ABC is now on the site), starring Jimmy Jewel and Ben Warris.

'Also in the cast were Jean Carson, who later went on to television success in America, Wally Boag, a charming balloon modeller and eccentric dancer from Portland, Oregon, the Godfrey Brothers, Muskani, a marvellous speciality act who literally turned himself inside out, and the wonderful singing legend, Joseph Locke. He was a tremendous draw, and the band had only to strike up the opening bars of *Hear my Song, Violetta* for the audience to go into paroxysms of delight.

'The follow spot would pick him up at the side of the stage as he carefully timed his entrance, enabling him to reach the centre microphone for the last few bars of music. Then, with those honey-toned top notes and that twinkle in his Irish eyes, he had the whole audience eating out of his hand.

'Another member of the company, who regularly stopped the show, was a small toothy kid in a little cotton frock and ankle strap shoes. She brought the house down every night, the minute she opened her mouth and began to sing an operatic aria from *La Traviata*. She was, of course, Julie Andrews.

'"Coconut Grove" was the brainchild of the legendary Robert Nesbit, who created a wonderful nightclub atmosphere within the confines of the auditorium. A samba band would greet you in the foyer as you booked your seats and bought your programme, creating an exciting mood before you even sat down.

'An open apron stage, complete with an illuminated glass run-out, and the orchestra to one side of the Proscenium, was an innovation that worked well and made the audience feel part of the show.

'The headliners themselves, Jewel and Warris, were in excellent form and performed their comedy routines to great effect — "Dick Turpin's Ride to York", the "Mustard Routine", ("Oh, so you don't like mustard! Now you're going to close down the factory and throw all those people out of work, just 'cos you don't like mustard!").or the "Timber" routine, when the pair dressed as lumberjacks sang "Timber, Timber, can't you hear us calling timber!", when half a ton of firewood falls on them from the flies.

'Another hilarious gag sees Ben trying to sell Jimmy a new type of pen that will write under water. A huge glass tank, full of water is wheeled on stage, and Jimmy is persuaded to remove most of his clothes; and get into the tank to sample the pen!

'Blackpool in 1949 was awash with stars. On the Central Pier, Frankie Howerd was top of the bill, with support from Ted and Barbara Andrews, (the parents of Julie Andrews).

'The Opera House was presenting 'Cheerful Charlie Chester' with his 'Stand Easy' gang — Ken Morris, Fred Ferrari, Len Marten, etc — and the fabulous Tiller Girls, with huge supporting cast.

'On the North Pier, in traditional elegant format, much loved by patrons over the years, was Lawrence Wright's production of comedy music and dancing of the highest order. Donald Peers and Norman Wisdom were at the Grand, with the former having a huge following at the time as a result of his success on the Hit Parade.

'*Annie Get Your Gun* at the Winter Gardens had come straight from the London Coliseum, with a full London company. There was a daily aqua show at the Derby Baths, an ice show down at the Pleasure Beach, twice-nightly variety at Feldman's Music Hall on the front, and if one felt like dancing the night away, the Winter Gardens and Tower Ballrooms provided romantic settings and music by all the top bands.'

What a Season!

Jimmy Tarbuck

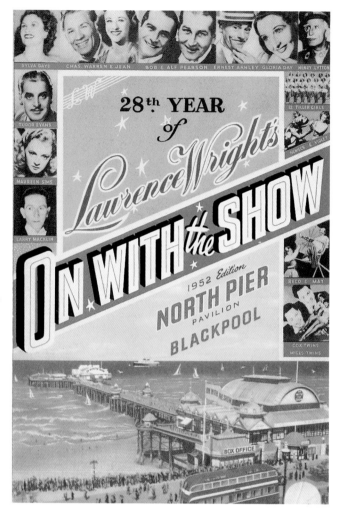

Just off the north-west coast, the **Isle of Man** has been a venue for entertainment since the early part of the century, with the Adeler and Sutton 'Pierrots' and later the 'Manx Mascots'. The Villa Marina has many visiting celebrity bands and the Douglas Palace was also a venue for variety shows.

Typical of the entertainment on offer there in 1949 was a Tom Arnold production at the Gaiety Theatre and Opera House in Douglas, the Island's principal town. It starred that popular duo Nat Mills and Bobbie, and was entitled 'Two Funny for Words'. The show was produced by Harry Bright, who had been responsible for a lot of shows at the London Palladium.

As well as Mills and Bobbie the show was packed with talent, the Maple Leaf Four, Desmond and Marks, who were a wonderful comedy knockabout and dancing act, Downey and Daye in a roller skating presentation, Dennis Martin, the Irish singer, and full supporting company and orchestra.

It is wonderful to know that 50 years later the Gaiety Theatre and Opera House has just been fully restored to its former glory and will be able to play its part in providing first class entertainment for holiday makers and residents alike.

My wife and I, with a couple of friends, were having a few days holiday in the **Torquay** area in 1961. The new Princess Theatre had just opened on the front, not far from the lovely old Pavilion. We booked up to see the Princess show, not only because it had a good cast, but we also wanted to see what the new theatre was like. What a show it was, with Tommy Cooper. Joan Regan (still looking as lovely as ever when I met her again in 1998), Morecambe and Wise, Canadian singer Edmund Hockridge, Ugo Garrido — a wonderful juggler — and a bevy of singers and dancers. It really was a show worthy of the new Torquay

Right: Sandy Powell and his wife Kay meet the Queen Mother after the show.

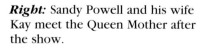

114

Don Ellis.

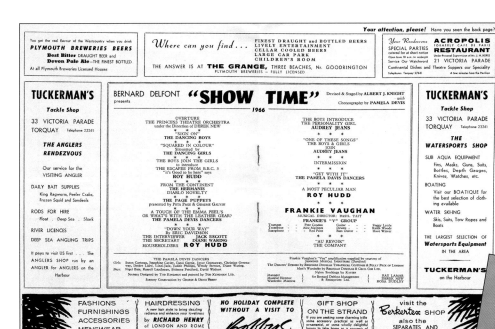
Far Left: 'On with the Show' was in its 28th year in 1952.

Left and Below: A Bernard Delfont 1966 production at Torquay featuring Roy Hudd and Frankie Vaughan.

PROGRAMME
ONE SHILLING

BERNARD DELFONT *presents* FRANKIE VAUGHAN *in* ShowTime at the PRINCESS THEATRE TORQUAY.

theatre. During that season Eric and Ernie had an offer to do their first series for commercial television, so they always had a sneaking feeling that Torquay was lucky for them, although they had played many other resorts, Bournemouth, Weymouth and Blackpool amongst them. They said that if you played Blackpool you were always talked about as 'having arrived'!

At the Pavilion Theatre in 1961 was the great comedy duo of Jimmy Jewel and Ben Warris, so the boys saw Jimmy and Ben and asked if they could give them some tips about doing a major TV series of 13 programmes. Jimmy and Ben's advice would always be worth listening to as they had years of experience in show business behind them. A major series requires a lot of material, even though they were going to have two good scriptwriters with them — Green and Hill.

Eric and Ernie later moved to the BBC where their success was even bigger. The boys starred in several Royal Variety performances at the Palladium and Ed Sullivan's famous American Chat Show. Later on they did a series of what Eric called 'bank raids' round the country — one-night stands which fitted in with their TV productions. They were now at the top of the light entertainment pyramid, a far cry from their early beginnings as bottom of the bill artistes in the not too fashionable smaller theatres, travelling the country on Sundays with the usual long waits at cold railway stations (at least waiting rooms were open then, when stations were manned by staff and not just video cameras without any film!).

What a tremendous amount of pleasure Morecambe and Wise have brought to millions of people over the years. We can put on a video of them when we're feeling depressed and just sit back and laugh. I wonder if our children will have the same feeling of amusement and sheer pleasure about some of our present-day comedy offerings in 25 or 30 years time!

Babbacombe, a small resort on the cliffs just a few miles from Torquay was the springboard for Roy Hudd's extraordinary career in show business. He did three seasons there in Brandon and Pounds 'Out of the Blue' starting in 1960.

Clive Dunn.

BRUCE FORSYTH

needs no introduction to residents and visitors, as this is his third season at Babbacombe. During the winter he has been starring at the Windmill Theatre, London W., and has also appeared on Television. He entered the profession at the age of 14 years, doing a Page Boy song and dance routine. He has appeared at the exclusive "Coconut Grove" Club, Savoy Hotel, Park Lane, Mayfair and Grosvenor House in Cabaret. A keen golfer, he has carried off many prizes in this field.

ELAINE CLIFFORD

was at Ilfracombe last season, and has just finished a busy winter in variety. She was in "No No Nanette," and has played a Middle East Tour entertaining the forces. On T.V. she has appeared in "Bid for Fame" and "Fancy Free." She has played Prince Charming in "Cinderella" and was in "Come to the Show" at Clacton and Bournemouth.

Telephone 88385

CONCERT HALL
BABBACOMBE

PROPRIETORS THE TORQUAY CORPORATION
ENTERTAINMENTS MANAGER A. F. ROBERTS
HOUSE SUPERVISOR I. D. BROWN

'**GAYTIME**'

THE SPARKLING SUMMER SHOW

7th SEASON

SUMMER SEASON 1957

Hedley Claxton's

IN 5 COMPLETE EDITIONS

Hedley Claxton who produces and presents "Gaytime" for the seventh season at Babbacombe is a Yorkshireman. He has had many years of experience in all branches of the profession, but regards summer shows as the ideal family entertainment. This season he is presenting companion companies at Cosy Nook, Newquay; Knightstone Theatre, Weston-super-Mare; The Cove Pavilion, Weston-super-Mare; and the Palace Theatre, Morecambe.

SOUVENIR PROGRAMME

PRICE 6d.

One of the Loveliest Spots in Torbay

The Concert Hall Babbacombe Downs

Permission to go to the seaside

Clive Dunn's career before *Dad's Army* may not be familiar to everyone, but his catchphrase as Corporal Jones to Captain Mainwaring —'Permission to speak Sir' — certainly is. Clive's professional career started well before World War II when he was just a lad, with a small part in the Will Hay comedy film *Good Morning Boys*. Later in 1937 he played a dancing frog and a flying dragon in *Where the Rainbow Ends*, a famous children's play of the time, at the Holborn Empire, London. He served in the Army during the war, spending some of it in Austria as a POW, and got back into civvy street in 1946, landing a job in pantomime in Birmingham.

He did his first summer season in 'Out of the Blue' in 1947 at the lovely little 'Cosy Nook' Theatre in Newquay. One evening the theatre caught fire; there was no one in the building at the time, but Clive was concerned that his one and only dress suit was in the dressing room close to the seat of the fire. Completely oblivious of his own safety, his one thought was to rescue his 'props'. Dashing into the smoke-filled building, he came out with his precious suit and a bundle of music, his face blackened, looking like Al Jolson! Clive was well on the road to learning his craft, and, as he himself has said, 'What better place to learn it than at the seaside?'

Clive's mother, Connie Clive, was a very talented and experienced summer revue performer in seasons with the 'Fol-de-Rols'. His father, Bobby Dunn, was also a star of summer shows, including seasons with the eccentric Reuben More. Clive's maternal grandfather, Frank Lynne was also a comedian, so there was plenty of talent in the family.

The postwar years saw Clive gaining experience, not only in the summer, but also the winter at the Players Theatre in London, where he was a regular guest artiste in their productions. During the 1950s he started doing television work while at the same time producing summer shows at Southwold and Cromer. The latter starred Graham Stark and Ronnie Corbett in their early summer season days and won an award for a seasonal show — that was when they used to recognise the quality of summer shows, as now is done with plays, television and films. Clive also played a season in Eric Ross's 'Dazzle' at the Esplanade Theatre, Bognor. More television work came his way and he was cast in *Bootsie and Snudge*, a long running series for commercial television. This was followed by appearances in Michael Bentine's *It's a Square World*, more TV work and films, until along came *Dad's Army* and even a hit record — *Grandad*.

Clive's dear wife, Cilla Morgan, is an experienced actress and has seldom been out of work — except to produce two lovely girls, Polly and Jessica. They really are a jolly family. May I suggest that you read a copy of Clive's autobiography *Permission to Speak*: it is very amusing and gives a very clear picture of entertainment after World War II.

Pavilion Theatre, Ilfracombe.

Left: Brucie's third season at Babbacombe was in 1957 — 'Didn't he do well!'

Right: Souvenir programme for the Pavilion Theatre, Ilfracombe.

Since then Roy has become a very good artiste in larger summer revues, leading the show. He is a major pantomime per-former, as well as writing and directing. He is the star of the longest run-ning BBC radio comedy series *The Hudd Lines*, and now his career has gone forward yet again as a featured player in films. He has no right to be so talented

Roy has very fond memories of the Babbacombe years and says it really taught him all the basics of the busi-ness. He recalls one hysterical moment (and there were several) with 'Out of the Blue' when Dickie Pounds, the lady producer insisted on the whole cast taking part in one of her ballets, of which she was very proud. They had a huge set depicting a volcano erupting with smoke and a little flame coming out of the top. The story of the ballet required one of the girls to be thrown into the volcano as a sacrifice. She was to be picked up by one of the boy dancers and carried upstage to her fate.

Unfortunately, the boy dancer was quite slight and the human sacrifice a big strapping girl. The poor lad was staggering about the stage with this girl in his arms try-ing to reach the volcano, which in the meantime had caught fire for real. Dickie Pounds was standing in the wings on one side of the stage, crying 'What are they doing, they're ruining my ballet!' On the other side

ILFRACOMBE
MUNICIPAL ENTERTAINMENTS

TELEPHONE: ILFRACOMBE 228

Souvenir Programme 6d.

Ronnie Brandon, co-producer in charge of pyrotechnics, put his head round the curtain and said, 'Ladies and Gentlemen, I'm very sorry but we will have to stop for a minute, the theatre's on fire!' Fortunately it was quickly extinguished and no one was hurt.

Roy and I met exact-ly 40 years ago in 1959, and during that time I have worked on several occasions with him in pan-tomime. He is enormous fun to be with, but at the same time a strict discipli-narian, which of course you have to be, particularly in pantomime, otherwise the comedy set pieces fall apart. We have even rehearsed the ad-libs — those moments of fun that the audience think are spontaneous — otherwise they become messy. I'm sure many people are unaware that Roy is a very good artist and a show-busi-ness historian, with several great books to his credit.

Still in Devon, in **Ilfracombe** to be precise, a town set amidst glorious coastal scenery, a young man was helping his parents run the Pavilion Theatre. This was many years ago now, and he did odd jobs backstage, painted the scenery and generally was a first rate dogsbody. He was filling in his time while awaiting his call up into the RAF. His ambition was to be a drummer, and he had been allowed to practise on the resident drummer's kit. In fact, he became a very good drummer, but fate was to intervene in the shape of the RAF gang shows, and the drums were put aside for the world of radio and, later, films. The young man's name? Peter Sellers.

Bournemouth's new entertainment centre.

Above: The Red Arrows over Bournemouth Pier Theatre.

Above Left: What a great farce for 1999!

Left: The Bournemouth entertainment centre at night.

Below Left: Note the production manager — David Croft, of *Dad's Army* fame.

The Promenade and Alexandra Gardens, Weymouth.

WEYMOUTH
PAVILION THEATRE
● GALA OPENING ●
THURSDAY, 14th JULY, at 8.0 p.m.
FOR THE SEASON

ALEXANDRA GARDENS THEATRE — WEYMOUTH

WEYMOUTH CORPORATION *presents*

DAVID HUGHES in

'MAKE MINE MUSIC'

SUNDAY, JULY 10th — 8.0 p.m.

PIER BANDSTAND
3.0 TWICE DAILY 7.30
'*Strike it Lucky*'
Featuring Your Host
HAROLD TAYLOR
"The Witty Wizard"
THE BIG GIVE AWAY SHOW

1. **OVERTURE**
Louis Mordish and His Music

2. **DAVID HUGHES**
introduces

3. **DAVE ALLEN**
New Star Comedian

4. **DEREK NEW**
Old Tunes for New

5. **DAVID HUGHES**
says 'How do you do' to . . .
BARBARA LEIGH
Radio and Television's favourite
Soprano

6. **DAVID HUGHES again**

7. **TOMMY REILLY**
International Harmonica Star

8. **DAVE ALLEN**
New Star Comedian

9. **DAVID HUGHES**
says 'Make Mine Music'

INTERVAL

THE QUEEN

Left: Weymouth Pavilion programme featuring David Hughes, who died far too young.

Below Left: The lovable Miles and Coy twins.

Below: 'Sunday Showtime' presents a 'new' comedian — one Jimmy Tarbuck — in 1964.

SANDOWN
PAVILION

SHANKLIN
THEATRE

SUNDAY, 28th JUNE

MICHAEL HAMILTON
and
BRYAN MICHIE

present

SUNDAY
SHOWTIME

A Concert of Celebrity Artistes from
Stage, T.V. and Radio

Guess who!

Right: The West Pier in
Brighton as it looks today.

Above and Left: Two Worthing
productions. 'Those Were the Days' and
the evergreen 'Twinkle'.

Peter Felgate.

Left: Eastbourne Lower Promenade, beach and pier.

Below Left: An Arthur Lane production from 1972 of 'The Golden Years of Music Hall' for the Royal Hippodrome, Eastbourne.

Below: Seen by two thousand people, twice daily: not bad eh?

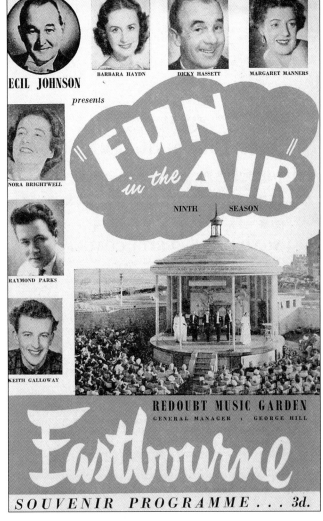

121

Benny Hill as he looked while performing at the Lido Theatre, Cliftonville, in 1950.

Above and Above Right: Two programmes for the De La Warr Pavilion, Bexhill-on-Sea.

Right: Two Margate summer show stars — the unmistakable Tommy Cooper and Larry Grayson.

Reg Varney with his vent doll 'Lookalike', seen at the
Lido, Cliftonville in 1950.

THE
ROYAL VICTORIA PAVILION
RAMSGATE

★

*The
Lupino Lane
Show*

★

SUMMER SEASON 1955

MARGATE CORPORATION ENTERTAINMENTS
WESTGATE PAVILION
General Manager and Licensee: J. D. Green, F.I.M.E.M.   Deputy Manager: A. D. EASTON, A.I.M.E.M.

CECIL JOHNSON
Presents
*Fancy
Free*

— 1962 EDITION —

A REFRESHING SHOW OF SONG, DANCE AND LAUGHTER

Programme

SIXPENCE

Above: Lupino Lane was
the star of the original
London production of *Me
and My Girl* in 1938.

Above Right: 'Fancy Free'
at the Westgate Pavilion,
Margate, in 1961.

Right: 'Take a tripp' with
Jack Tripp.

Far Right: The Cliffs
Pavilion Southend in 1974.
From left to right: front
row, Billy Dainty, the
Karlin Sisters and Edmund
Hockeridge; back row,
Tommy and Beryl Wallis at
right.

LIDO
Theatre MARGATE

1977

BUNNY BARON *presents*

JACK
TRIPP
in

take a tripp

123

The author stars at the Pavilion Theatre, Wellington Pier, Great Yarmouth. It was great working with the girls.

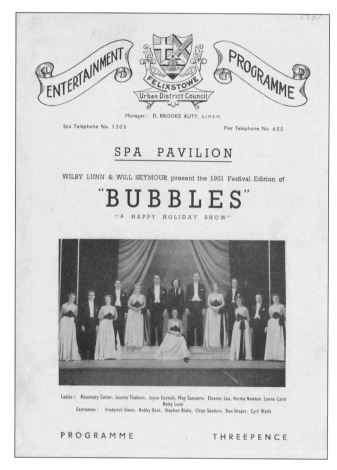

Above: 'Bubbles' at the Felixstowe Spa Pavilion in 1951.

Above Right: 'Out of the Blue', Felixstowe. The cast includes Terry Scott, Hugh Lloyd, John Boulter, and Beryl and Tom Plummer.

Right: Clacton Pier as it looked in the 1930s.

The Gorleston Pavilion today.

Above: 1950s programme for 'Between Ourselves' at the Arcadia Lowestoft — 'The summer show of distinction'.

Above Right: Gorleston Pavilion souvenir programme from 1973.

Right: The Promenade Gorleston-on-Sea. The Pavilion Theatre is the large red brick building with pale blue towers in the background.

Tom Howell's 'Opieros', Great Yarmouth.

Above and Bottom: The changing face of Great Yarmouth's entertainment — from the 'Opieros' to the Beatles.

Right and Below: Britannia Pier, Great Yarmouth, in 1906 and 1912.

Above: Ronnie really was a big stage and recording star in 1955 when he appeared at the Wellington Pier Pavilion, Great Yarmouth.

Left: An early seaside appearance of the Beatles.

The demolition of the famous Skegness Arcadia.

Above and Left: Some East Coast attractions — who could resist the delights of 'Holiday Carnival' at the Futurist Theatre, Scarborough, or 'A Night at the Music Hall' at the Spa Theatre. Whitby?

Russ Conway

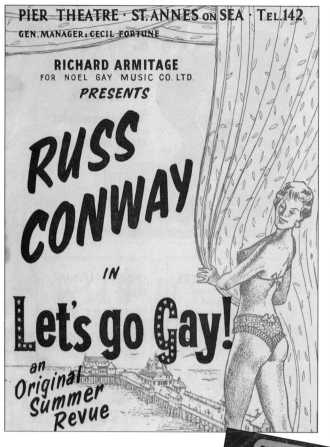

Above: Russ Conway's first summer season show.

Above Right: Charlie Chester and the 'Stand Easy' gang.

Centre Right: The original Grand Theatre, Blackpool in 1948. It looks rather different now — see page 129.

Right: Two Blackpool show programmes: 'Sky High' at the new Opera House with Charlie Chester starring, and the Silver Jubilee of 'On With the Show' at the North Pier in 1949.

Charlie Chester.

Above Left: Charlie Chester and the 'Stand Easy' gang. Just as popular live as they were on radio in 1949.

Above: The magnificent interior of the Grand, Blackpool . . .

Left: . . . and their great Blackpool show.

Left: Arthur Wolsley with 'Charlie Brown'.

Right: Peter Goodwright, impressionist supreme.

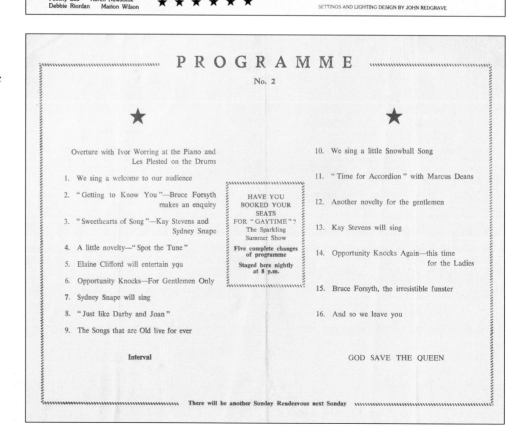

Babbacombe Theatre
General Manager (for the Corporation)
A. F. ROBERTS
Telephone 88385
House Supervisor
I. D. BROWN

ERIC ROSS presents...

The DAZZLE Show

PROGRAMME   SIXPENCE

Above: Another 'Dazzle' venue.

Above Right: Babbacombe programme from 1981 featuring the Eurovision Song for Europe winner, Dana.

Right: A Sunday in Babbacombe with 'Brucie'.

ED & DIRECTED BY
REDGRAVE
D BY
NY BISHOP

OVERTURE
JOHNNY WILTSHIRE SHOWBAND
MUSICAL DIRECTOR **DAVE GOLD**

"That's Entertainment".... **NEW FORMATION**
introduce ...
STELLA & BAMBOS
ARTHUR WORSLEY
and.... **PETER GOODWRIGHT**

"Latin Flavour".... **STELLA & BAMBOS**

NEW FORMATION.....'Bond'Together

"Turn Me Round Son".....
ARTHUR WORSLEY
with
CHARLIE BROWN
PAVLOV'S PUPPETS

Jan Lynton's New Formation
Felicity Lea   Karen Newsome
Debbie Riordan   Marion Wilson

HOLIDAY SPECTACULAR

ENTRACTE
JOHNNY WILTSHIRE SHOWBAND
"Colour Mix"....**NEW FORMATION**

PETER GOODWRIGHT
★
DANA
★
"That's All"......**FULL COMPANY**

FOR HOLIDAY SPECTACULAR COMPANY
Theatre Manager...............MARGARET BROOKS
Production Manager..............TONY GARDNER
Scenic Supervisor..................JOHN GARDNER
Wardrobe Supervisor............ZENA GARDNER
Musical Arranger..................PAUL VINCENT
Stage Manager.........CHRISTOPHER GARDNER
SETTINGS AND LIGHTING DESIGN BY JOHN REDGRAVE

INTERVAL

PROGRAMME
No. 2

Overture with Ivor Worring at the Piano and
Les Plested on the Drums

1. We sing a welcome to our audience
2. "Getting to Know You"—Bruce Forsyth makes an enquiry
3. "Sweethearts of Song"—Kay Stevens and Sydney Snape
4. A little novelty—"Spot the Tune"
5. Elaine Clifford will entertain you
6. Opportunity Knocks—For Gentlemen Only
7. Sydney Snape will sing
8. "Just like Darby and Joan"
9. The Songs that are Old live for ever

Interval

HAVE YOU BOOKED YOUR SEATS FOR "GAYTIME"? The Sparkling Summer Show
Five complete changes of programme
Staged here nightly at 8 p.m.

10. We sing a little Snowball Song
11. "Time for Accordion" with Marcus Deans
12. Another novelty for the gentlemen
13. Kay Stevens will sing
14. Opportunity Knocks Again—this time for the Ladies
15. Bruce Forsyth, the irresistible funster
16. And so we leave you

GOD SAVE THE QUEEN

There will be another Sunday Rendezvous next Sunday

130

Berryman's 'Evening Stars'.

Left: The entrance to Teignmouth Pier.

Below: John Berryman's 'Evening Stars'.

Bottom: Moira Lister advertising Newquay in Cornwall, before she became a famous actress.

Below Left: 1970 Victoria Pavilion programme featuring 'Showtime'.

VICTORIA
PAVILION - ILFRACOMBE

SHOWTIME
'70

Programme 6d.

Torquay harbour — the centre of the English Riviera.

Right: Eric and Ernie brought sunshine wherever they went.

Below Right: A bevy of great Fol-de-Rol artistes including that dear chap Leslie Crowther.

Below: The dear old Gaity Theatre in Minehead. A David Graves production from 1951.

Another angle of Torquay harbour with the Pavilion in the top right corner.

Left: The Princess Theatre, Torquay, is built on the site of the old Princess Pier. Today stars such as Joe Pasquale can be seen there.

Below Left: A favourite bill topper — Tom o'Connor.

Below: A good three-penny worth!

133

The Celtic Fringe

SCOTLAND

Scotland has always had a great tradition of entertainment, with a consistent flowering of musical talent, dancing and comedy as well as some wonderful singers.

From the early 18th century there were little touring shows, with their portable fit-up theatres — 'geggies' or 'gegs' as they were known. Does the modern word 'gig' meaning a one-night stand or part of a travelling schedule of performances, derive from this I wonder?

Scottish entertainers, like some wine, did not always travel well, and they found it difficult to be appreciated and sometimes even understood outside their homeland. One notable exception was Harry Lauder, who became one of the highest paid and most successful Scottish entertainers and performed all over the world to great acclaim. He also received a knighthood — a rarity among Scots performers.

Other Scottish names — such as Tommy Lorne, Will Fyfe, Jimmy Logan, Stanley Baxter, Duncan Macrae, Andy Stewart, Robert Wilson, Jack Radcliffe, Kenneth MacKellar, Moira Anderson, Rikki Fulton, Jack Milroy, Johnny Beattie and Calum Kennedy — are all testimony to the Scottish tradition. All started their careers in small shows up and down the country and around the coasts. They also often took their shows out to the Highlands and Islands, to remote villages where they performed in small halls and institutes which were always packed to the rafters with folk making the journey from far and wide to see their favourite artistes. This tradition still continues today, and Billy Connolly is among many who keep it alive and vibrant.

However, there are two venues that have a premier position in Scottish seaside entertainment. One is the Gaiety Theatre, Ayr, run by the famous Popplewell family, the other the Beach Pavilion, Aberdeen, synonymous with the name of Harry Gordon.

The city of Aberdeen on the northeast coast of Scotland, the Beach Pavilion and Harry Gordon are names forever linked together in the history of seaside entertainment. Harry was born in the city in 1893 and made his first appearance on the professional variety stage in 1910 at the old Empire Theatre in George Street (now the offices of the Northern Friendly Society). Following this he spent two seasons with 'Monty's Pierrots' at

Right: The 'Rebels' Carnoustie, 1925. In the centre of the photo is Cissie Cave, the mother of Billy Moore.

Harry Gordon.

Left: 'Gaiety Whirl', Ayr, 1959. The cast includes in the centre Jack Milroy, Gwen Overton, Clive Stock and The Plummers.

Stonehaven and in 1915 was a member of 'Collins's Pierrots' at Burntisland in Fife at a salary of £3 per week. Although there were a few local humourists and Pierrots performing alfresco along the beach at the beginning of the century, the weather in that part of Scotland was not conducive to open-air entertainment, and with that in mind a far-seeing town council built a more permanent structure of wood with a corrugated iron roof — the Beach Pavilion — under the direction of a comedian and Master of Ceremonies, David Thomson. Here in 1913 Harry began his long association with the venue.

After serving for a time in France during World War I as a non-combatant (his eyesight was so poor they daren't let him have a rifle!), Harry once more took up the reins at the Beach Pavilion, and gradually the shows were modernised and improved into the slick, clean, family summer revues that were to become so associated with the town of Aberdeen. These shows were so successful that in 1928 a new theatre was built to replace the old wooden one and 'Harry Gordon and his Entertainers' became a firmly established part of the scenery.

Harry Gordon also collaborated with Archie Hyslop who wrote so many wonderful lyrics for Harry's vocal character studies, as well as being the inventor of 'The Laird of Inversnecky' from that imaginary village 'somewhere near Aberdeen'. (It became so real in the minds of visitors to the city that they would often enquire at the local bus station how to get there!)

The shows at the Beach Pavilion went from strength to strength and the introduction of 'London Guest Artistes' was a popular innovation. The famous names of the 1930s were such people as Jack Warner, Anne Zeigler and Webster Booth, Flotsam and Jetsam, Flanagan and Allan, Bob and Alf Pearson, Anona Winn and Vanessa Lee. In the 1920s Josie Collins and Gertrude Lawrence also visited the Pavilion as did Billy Mayerl the pianist, and the Western Brothers, Kenneth and George, who were probably the first to be lured away from the London Cabaret Circuit to appear in Aberdeen.

On Saturday matinee days a large table would be set up in one of the dressing rooms and a sumptuous tea laid out for all the artistes. This created a truly jolly family atmosphere that the performers found hard to resist.

In 1940, with the war in full swing and the constant threat of air raids, etc., Harry finally said goodbye to the Pavilion. In subsequent years it played host to a number of stars. Julie Andrews and The Beverley Sisters appeared there in the early 1950s and Morecambe and Wise did a

The Pierrots, Girvan, 1909.

The Beach Pavilion,
Aberdeen, the
popular Harry
Gordon's venue.

stint there as resident compères. Finally, the building became a restaurant and it is now split up with the addition of a cafe. Many of those who dine there are totally unaware of the colourful history that surrounds them.

Meanwhile in 1928, on the west coast in Ayr, a Yorkshireman called Ben Popplewell bought an old building that had been in use as a theatre since 1902. He rebuilt the theatre, calling it the Gaiety, and started putting in star names such as Florrie Ford, Will Fyfe, etc., in a show by the name of *Gaiety Whirl*. Its slogan was 'The Family Theatre, Run by a Family, For the Family' and such was its success that everyone who was anyone in Scottish entertainment played there. 'The Whirl' celebrated its diamond jubilee in 1990, with Johnny Beattie and the Alexander Brothers headlining. The theatre suffered a fire in 1955, and in 1973 nearly ended up as a Tesco's car park, but thanks to the efforts of many former 'Gaiety Whirlers', (in particular Andy Stewart and Jimmy Logan) the Gaiety was saved from such a dire fate, and it is now a civic trust.

Elsewhere in Scotland seaside entertainment flourished — particularly on the Clyde coast in the 1920s and 1930s with the famous paddle steamers taking the thousands of holidaymakers 'doon the watter' to Largs, Prestwick and Rothesay on the beautiful Isle of Bute. The Winter Gardens on the huge esplanade seated some 1,200 people, and played host to the 'Rothesay Entertainers', among them Jack Antony, Tommy Morgan and Robert Wilson.

Other resorts that did well were Dunoon, Dunbar, North Berwick, Gourock, Arbroath and Saltcoats. So much so that in the 1930s the well-known producer, Ross Bowie, had 14 different summer shows running on the coasts in Scotland. So popular were these seaside shows in the 1930s that the management of the Kings Theatre, Glasgow, decided to copy the idea of a resident company of versatile performers, but with a resident orchestra, and more elaborate scenery and costumes. They would go on to present a series of memorable revues called 'Half Past Eight' with the cream of Scottish theatre, including many English artistes. This spawned a later version, 'Five Past Eight' at the Alhambra with many well-known names in the cast list, indeed many who had made their first appearance beside the seaside or on the pier.

Colwyn Bay Pier Pavilion.

WALES

The 'Land of Song' certainly has produced some great stars, notably Gladys Morgan, who was not only a stage performer but a big radio name in such shows as *Welsh Rarebit*. Ivor Emmanuel was another fine singer and actor. (Remember him in *Zulu* with Michael Caine?). Tom Jones and Shirley Bassey were wonderful ambassadors for their country all over the world — as was that lovely man, Harry Secombe, the 'arch-Goon' himself, with a fine tenor voice and endearing sense of fun.

Although one has to admit that the north coast of Wales has been the premier centre of entertainment in the resorts, there are other areas that have been popular through the years. Aberystwith had early visiting pierrot companies, and Swansea, with its beautifully restored Empire Theatre, has always presented very good productions. The New Theatre in Cardiff is now refurbished and become home to the Welsh National Opera.

However it is Llandudno which has been the focal point in Welsh entertainment since before the turn of the century. Then the pier had a grand pavilion which provided concerts with the most celebrated artistes of the day — the world-renowned Italian tenor Gigli, conductor Barberolli, Paul Robeson, and many others. The Pier Pavilion Orchestra in 1927 was led by David McCallum, the father of film star David. In the 1950s Bernard Delfont took over the Pier Pavilion, presenting summer shows, then he was followed by someone who was little known outside show business circles — Harold Fielding, who produced shows all over the country under the title *Music for the Millions*. This was in the mid-1950s, and Fielding chose all the top artistes of the day — concert pianist Semprini, Bob and Alf Pearson, Beryl Reid, Jon Pertwee, the Radio Revellers, Russ Conway, and not forgetting Saveen, a brilliant ventriloquist working with two dogs, one a puppet, the other a real one!

I must mention an incident when I was doing some stooging for my cousin, Jon, when he was appearing in one of Fielding's shows at the Winter Gardens Margate. We went to see what the opposition were doing at the lovely old Victorian Hippodrome there. We only had time to see the first half of the show, which was called *Hot from Harlem*. One of the acts was a young girl who made us all sit up the moment she started to sing. What a voice! Her name, very small on the programme, was Shirley Bassey.

Another fabulous act that played Llandudno for Fielding was the 'Beverley Sisters'. The delightful 'Bevs' played all the other major resorts with *Music for the Millions* including Great Yarmouth, Southsea, Blackpool and Bournemouth. The trio was also very popular in America and scored there with their hit records. They very soon became a hot property, and quite rightly so, their sheer professionalism and the hard work they put in before a performance, which is so evident when you see them, makes you respect their dedication. It is no wonder that the girls have remained at the top for so long.

Colwyn Bay Pier and Pavilion as they looked in around the 1920s.

Clive Stock.

There was an open air theatre called 'Happy Valley' in Llandudno for many years. It was just a wooden stage with a canopy. It was always a successful venue, firstly run by a chap called Waldini, then later the comedian Alex Munro, the father of film star Janet, who unfortunately died far too young. In 1969, the singer Clive Stock joined forces with a well known organist, Robinson Cleaver, to present the shows at the nearby Pier Pavilion, Llandudno, as well as also at the Arcadia. They staged celebrity concerts on Sundays and summer shows at both venues with a host of well known artistes from television and radio. They also presented concerts at the Palace Theatre, Morecambe.

When Clive and Robbie decided to call it a day in 1982, they really had catered for all tastes at the resort and their productions had broken box office records at the same time as bringing a great deal of pleasure to a lot of people.

In 1983, Clive Stock took over as general manager of the Aberconway Centre. His early career had been as a singer in West End musicals, then he had many successful years in a double act with his wife, Gwen Overton, playing all the big seaside dates and London concert engagements.

It is worth mentioning now the history of the Arcadia Theatre in Llandudno. It was built before the turn of the century by an eccentric

Above: Colwyn Bay Pier. In early days it was the scene of the debut performance of the boy soprano David Ivor Davies — later better known as Ivor Novello.

Left: Llandudno Pavilion as it looked in 1959.

Above Right: Bob and Alf Pearson in their youth.

Far Right: 'Twinkle' at Llandudno in summer 1964.

Bob and Alf getting older.

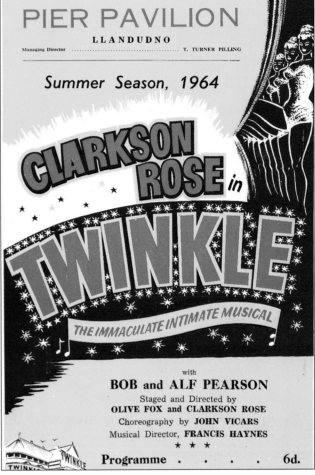

musician called Jules Riviere. It was originally called the Victoria Palace and then later the Hippodrome, but this three-sided building was in reality used not only for celebrity concerts, but for ice skating and, would you believe it, motor racing! In 1915 Will Catlin arrived at the resort from Scarborough to present his pierrots and concert parties, and later his revues — Catlin's 'Showtime'. He renamed the building 'Arcadia' after his own theatre in the Yorkshire resort. He was once again as successful here as he had been in Scarborough. The Grand Theatre (just behind the Arcadia) was used by the BBC during the last war when a lot of the BBC staff were evacuated from London to that part of the country .

Let us now move to nearby Colwyn Bay with its famous pier. It has had a few disastrous moments in its time, notably two fires earlier in this century, but after rebuilding it was business as usual. There was also a small

theatre on it called the Bijou, which was also gutted by fire. However, the pier carried on business with various entertainments in the new pavilion at the shore end.

Colwyn Bay also had early pierrot troupes presented by Will Catlin and other managements, and the final summer shows on the pier were the 'Bouquets' presented by Betty Lunn. Perhaps one of the most memorable events early in the century was the Colwyn Bay debut of boy soprano David Ivor Davies, with his mother, Clara Novello Davies. The world would hear a great deal more of young master Davies, or Ivor Novello as he was to become. He was the composer of *Glamourous Nights*, *The Dancing Years*, *Perchance to Dream* and many, many more, and was the greatest tunesmith of light music this century without doubt.

The pier at Colwyn Bay is now owned by Mike and Anne Paxman, who sold up everything to buy it, and they

Llandudno Pier as shown on the farewell programme.

Right: . . . and in an early photograph.

Below: A Catlin production.

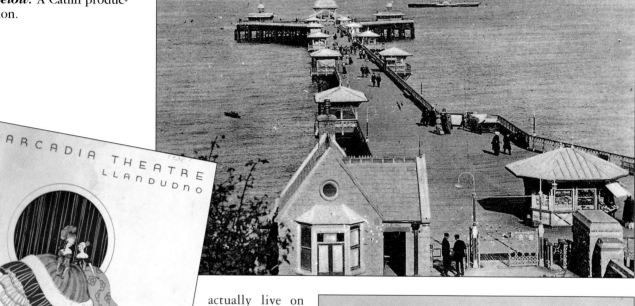

ARCADIA THEATRE
LLANDUDNO

*Catlin's
Summer
Follies*

actually live on it. At the Shore End there is a cafe and shops, and as funds become available they will tackle the great task of restoration ahead of them. It is unfortunate that their lottery grant application was turned down, but perhaps they will be luckier next time; they certainly deserve it, and we wish them well.

If you think I was forgetting Rhyl, well I haven't. One of Will Catlin's daughters (Gladys) married a superb female impersonator called Billy Manders and he took over the amphitheatre at Rhyl and called his productions the 'Quaintesques'. His shows ran for 29 years from 1921 onwards, and won a national newspaper competition for the best concert party in the British Isles.

What a marvellous theatrical history this part of Wales has had!

Right: The farewell programme.

PIER & PAVILION
LLANDUDNO
General Manager & Secretary : T. TURNER PILLING

Farewell
Programme

Rhyl, 1963.

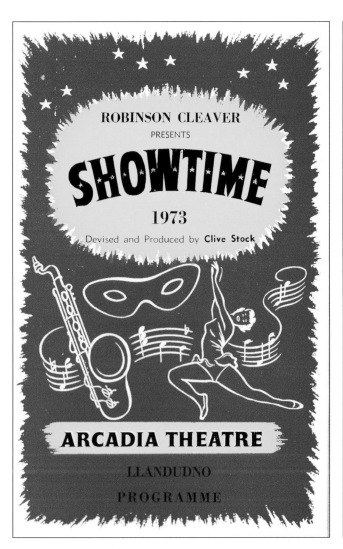

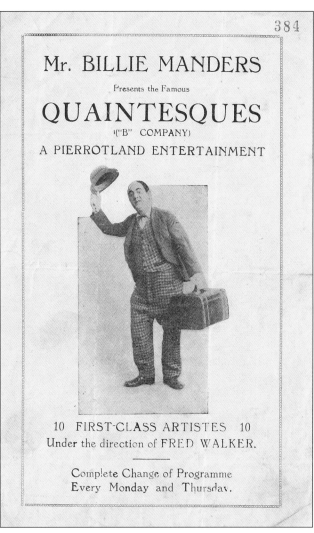

Above Left: A Stock/
Cleaver production.

Above: Billie really knew
the business inside-out.

Left: A sunny day on the
Promenade, Aberystwyth
c. 1959.

Appendices

THE CHARITABLE ORGANISATIONS

People constantly ask me about our business, particularly what happens to retired performers, those who haven't been amongst the big earners — are they looked after?

This is quite a reasonable question and I'll try to answer it. Firstly, actors and actresses can, and usually do, just carry on working, some of them into quite an advanced age. There are character parts for them to play and, as one of them said to me, 'as long as I can stand up I'll carry on'.

The situation can be quite different for comedians, singers, jugglers, magicians, etc. In fact the solo performers have to put away their props because of the nature of their work. Many of the seaside entertainers who were the backbone of so many shows but never hit the big time, do occasionally need help, and the theatrical charities which those same artistes have supported in the past are able in turn give them help when it is needed.

These charities are few in number and I will mention some here: the Equity Benevolent Fund, the General Theatrical Fund, the Water Rats, the CAA, the Entertainment Artistes Benevolent, and the Actors Charitable Trust. The latter two also look after Brinsworth House and Denville Hall, retirement homes for actors and actresses, and those who still live in their own homes but need a little help every now and again, perhaps to assist with their phone bills, etc.

The EABF looks after the solo performers in the light entertainment business and their retirement home, complete with a specialised nursing unit, is Brinsworth House in Twickenham. I am on the committee of the EABF and I can tell you the care that is offered there is wonderful, the whole atmosphere is one of a great big family. The fund also, as with other charities, gives support to those still living at home. The EABF is administered by Peter Elliott and his marvellous team. The fund has been supported by the Royal Family since 1912, when a Royal Variety Performance in the presence of King George V and Queen Mary helped to provide some money for the less fortunate in our business. This continued right up until the present day and hopefully will continue — the present Queen and the Queen Mother are patrons of the fund and take a great interest, as does Prince Charles. All the funds work together for the lesser known artistes who year after year spent seasons at the seaside — often for little financial reward — keeping audiences happy.

Peter Elliott has been a performer all his life, so he knows the business very well indeed, as well as those who have worked in it.

Peter Elliott in his early days had one funny experience in Scotland in a small show in Ayrshire. The theatre was really more of a hut than anything else. The principle comedian was one Tommy Hood (well known in Scotland at that time) who thought he should be doing a better date than in the humble 'Hut'.

During one performance Tommy got really cross because something wasn't set on a table in a sketch and walked off stage in a huff. The pianist, a very nervous man at whom Tommy was always shouting, was told to play something while the problem was sorted out. This he did with gusto, playing popular choruses that the audience picked up on and a good sing-song started. Vince, the pianist, got more and more excited with the reaction and was eventually standing up and egging the audience on to sing louder, which they did. Nothing could stop the

Left: Brinsworth House, Twickenham.

Right: Not all artistes can be as successful as that great entertainer Arthur Askey.

142

Theatre Royal Bournemouth programme from 1956.

enjoyment. This was Vince's big moment, but meanwhile Tommy Hood, who was now ready to continue, couldn't carry on because he couldn't be heard above the singing. He walked to the front of the stage and shouted as loud as he could at Vince, *'You're sacked as from now.'* Vince got up and walked out, followed by half the audience still singing merrily. Poor old Vince could have done with a little charitable support, I should think, in the ensuing few days, but he had at least enjoyed himself in the 'Hut' on that day.

Concert Artistes Association

At the turn of the century many music societies, city livery companies and masonic lodges were holding regular functions where they wanted to engage professional entertainers, and thus were providing work for the new breed of singers, musicians, light comedians, magicians and monologuists — as distinct from the more robust and earthy performers who filled the bill at the music hall. Apart from their winter work, such artistes formed the backbone of the summer seaside concert parties. The CAA was formed in 1897 to administer a benevolent fund to alleviate distress and hardship among such members of the concert profession, the maintenance of adequate fees for artistes, and the formation of a club for members. The CAA also provided a meeting place to relax after fulfilling an engagement in town, or to meet up after a long season by the sea to catch up on all the news and gossip. It was also an opportunity to meet agents and often secure work.

Later, after the association moved into its premises in Bedford Street in the heart of theatreland (still its current home) Monday night concerts were arranged. These always included one or two introductory performances by new or untried hopefuls, to show what they could do in front of an audience.

My own 'Monday Night Introductory' secured me a booking in the summer show in Gorleston in 1955 — my first steps into this profession.

The association now has a thriving membership of not only concert artistes, but many actors from stage and television and West End shows who like to drop in to the club for a drink and a sandwich to relax after their evening performance. There is also a large lunchtime membership drawn from the many businesses and trades in the Covent Garden area.

Its past presidents — and I have had the honour to be among them — include some illustrious names: Norman Long, Elsie and Doris Waters, Arthur Askey, Susette Tarri, Jack Warner, Anne Zeigler and Webster Booth, Cyril Fletcher, Owen Brannigan, Hugh Lloyd, Cardew Robinson, David Nixon, Leslie Crowther, Hubert Gregg, Jimmy Perry, Roy Hudd, Brian Murphy, Ruth Madoc, Carmen Silvera and Pamela Cundell.

For further information can I recommend a great little book all about the CAA written by Larry Parker, himself a past president and active member. It is a fascinating account, full of interest with a foreword by Julie Andrews, herself a summer-season artiste in her youth, whose parents, Ted and Barbara Andrews, were long-time members.

But — What Do You Do In The Winter? by Larry Parker
CAA Bookshop, 20 Bedford Street, London, WC2E 9HP

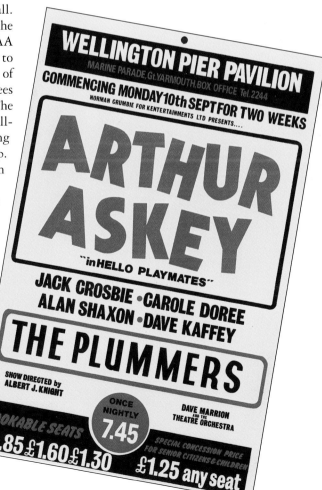

The West Pier in Brighton, taken in 1995.

NATIONAL PIERS SOCIETY

The National Piers Society may not be a widely known organisation outside the seaside resorts, but it is gradually gaining recognition and a wider audience all the time, and quite rightly so

The members have put in a tremendous amount of time and effort in their support for the magnificent piers around our coasts, especially with the organisations set up to rescue and maintain them, helping to keep for future generations that very British institution, the seaside pier. Of course, it would not be practical to try to reclaim all of the remaining structures still in evidence, and the society would be the first to admit it.

However, there is something unique about a pier, and every child and adult at some time or another has associated it with a summer holiday by the sea. I am one of them, having worked on several in my time.

The society has already achieved much in the process of restoration. Bangor, in North Wales, is a unique structure with some wonderful architecture. The Clevedon Pier in Somerset is another, not the prettiest perhaps, but still outstanding in design. Penarth in South Wales is another to benefit and the glorious West Pier at Brighton has recently received some funding and work has begun on restoring it to its former glory.

The theatre at the sea end of the West Pier is actually still intact, apart from the seating, and must hold many memories for the artistes who played there in the various repertory companies between the wars. The current owners are the West Pier Trust, and although the structure has been terribly neglected in the past, they are now embarking on a programme of restoration which will also see the Concert Hall, the lovely building in the middle of the pier, brought back to its former glory. My wife and I both played there in 1965 and 1966 respectively and what a marvellous time we had. I can't wait to walk along the deck again and revive old memories!

The Birnbeck Pier at Weston-super-Mare is also being given some much needed attention and sponsorship. For a small donation towards restoration, some metres of decking can be purchased and engraved with the donor's name, the wood coming from a managed renewable source, so as not to damage the rain forests any further.

Southport is a listed structure and that too has been allotted funds, only half of what is needed admittedly, but at least it's a start!

The folk in Yorkshire will be pleased to know that Saltburn Pier — the only one remaining on that part of the coast — is undergoing extensive restoration, while on the south coast Hastings Pier is looking for a buyer, although the one at Bognor Regis has unfortunately had its grant application turned down.

If you want a story of dedication, then the restoration of Colwyn Bay's Victoria Pier must be it. After several changes of ownership and the sword of Damocles hanging over it, a Mr and Mrs Paxman decided to buy it and sold off their own home and practically everything else in order to save this lovely pier. They now live on it and quite a lot of the shore end has been put to good use with a cafe and several small shops. The rest of the pier remains closed, as an application for lottery funding has been turned down. How disappointing for the Paxmans, having given up so much in order to keep this lovely structure open.

I have a feeling, however, that all is not lost. People like the Paxmans are difficult to keep down and I'm sure will continue to fulfil their dreams.

Finally, I would like to acknowledge the great help given to me by Anthony Wills — much appreciated.

If you would like to know more about the National Piers Society and receive their quarterly magazine, you will be well rewarded, and the Society will be delighted to have your support.

For details write to:
The Membership Secretary,
82 Aldington Close,
Lodge Park,
REDDITCH,
Hereford and Worcester,
B98 7NF.